CANDY
EXPERIMENTS

2

LORALEE LEAVITT

Andrews McMeel
Publishing

Kansas City · Sydney · London

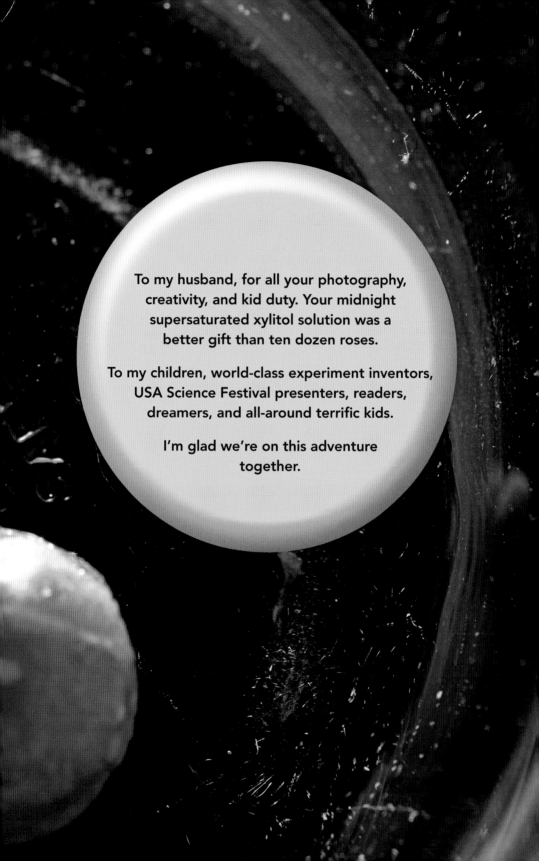

To my husband, for all your photography, creativity, and kid duty. Your midnight supersaturated xylitol solution was a better gift than ten dozen roses.

To my children, world-class experiment inventors, USA Science Festival presenters, readers, dreamers, and all-around terrific kids.

I'm glad we're on this adventure together.

CONTENTS

Acknowledgments . . . **vii**

Introduction . . . **ix**

Experiment Tips . . . **x**

Candy Experiment Science Fair Projects . . . **xii**

ACIDS AND BASES . . . 1

Color-Changing Gummies . . . **2**

Can You Taste pH? . . . **4**

Fizzing Soda Candy . . . **6**

Acid Dissolving Test . . . **8**

Acid Attack . . . **10**

DISSOLVE . . . 15

Stirring Race . . . **16**

How Much Dissolves? . . . **18**

How Fast Does It Dissolve? . . . **20**

The Ghost Lollipop . . . **22**

Half-and-Half Peeps . . . **23**

Does a Gummi Worm Dissolve? . . . **24**

Vanishing Cotton Candy . . . **26**

The Cotton Candy Sponge . . . **28**

Candy Ice Tunnels . . . **30**

MELT . . . 33

"Chocolate" Conversation Hearts . . . **34**

Puddle O' Peeps . . . **36**

Gulping Gummies . . . **38**

Gummi Worm Jell-O . . . **39**

JUST ADD (OR REMOVE) WATER . . . 41

Wormy Cotton Candy . . . **42**

Easter Grass Spaghetti . . . **44**

Seize Chocolate . . . **46**

Pale Chocolate . . . **48**

Dyeing Gummi Worms . . . **50**

Saltwater Gummi Soak . . . **52**

Shatter Peeps . . . **54**

Can You Fry a Cadbury Egg? . . . **56**

DENSITY . . . 59

Shrink Cotton Candy . . . **60**

Can You Float a Sunken Candy Bar? . . . **62**

Swimming Gummi Frog . . . **64**

Tootsie Rising . . . **66**

Swimming Pop Rocks . . . **68**

Pop Rocks Density Layers . . . **70**

FREE THE BUBBLES . . . 73

Flip the Gummi Ring . . . **74**

Bubbles and Hearts . . . **75**

Warty Licorice . . . **76**

Crush Pop Rocks . . . **77**

Puffy Pop Rocks . . . **78**

Unbubbling Pop Rocks . . . **80**

Pop Rocks Bubble Trap . . . **82**

Popcorn Pop Rocks . . . **84**

Soda Geyser Showdown . . . **86**

Diving Candy . . . **90**

LIGHT ... 93

Can Sugar Water Bend Light? . . . **94**
Sugar Water Swirls . . . **96**
Invisible Licorice . . . **98**
Cotton Candy Stained Glass . . . **100**
Ghostly Gummies . . . **103**
Vanishing Gummies . . . **104**
The Gummi Gecko . . . **106**
Translucent Taffy . . . **107**
Turn Pixy Stix Translucent . . . **108**
Melt Chocolate with a Magnifying Glass . . . **110**

CRYSTALS ... 113

Un-Brown Sugar . . . **114**
Chocolate Sawdust . . . **116**
Ice Crystals . . . **118**
Candy Diamonds . . . **120**
Instant Crystallization . . . **122**

JUST FOR FUN ... 125

Jousting Peeps . . . **126**
Sugar-Free Tic Tacs? . . . **127**
Marshmallow Bottle Launcher . . . **128**
Do Mint and Orange Mix? . . . **130**
Do Chocolate Peanuts Make Chocolate Peanut Butter? . . . **132**
Cotton Candy Sugar Showdown . . . **134**
What Kind of Candy Lasts Longest? . . . **136**
Shatter Frozen Marshmallows . . . **138**

Index . . . **142**

ACKNOWLEDGMENTS

Many thanks to Michael Corey, biochemist, and Jonathan Stapley, carbohydrate chemist, who reviewed experiments and clarified my understanding of innumerable chemical concepts.

Additional thanks to Bill Fredericks, the "Chocolate Man," for an in-depth phone call about chocolate, crystals, and color; Joel H. Berg, DDS, MS, dean of the University of Washington School of Dentistry, for answers about acid and tooth enamel; Day L. Bassett, PhD, for osmosis and fluid dynamics explanations; biochemist Lorin R. Thompson, for conversations about starch and science fairs; Teisha Rowland of sciencebuddies.org, for long conversations at the USA Science and Engineering Festival (USASEF) about science projects, and www.sciencebuddies.org for science fair project guidelines; Emma of www.science-sparks.com for the idea of putting Pop Rocks in oil; C&H Consumer Affairs, for their e-mail response summarizing the process of sugar refining; and Impact Confections, www.candyfavorites.com, and www.temptationcandy.com for donating candy to the cause of science.

Special thanks to the several families who tested experiments, rated ideas, caught errors, and clarified instructions.

And finally, thanks to my family members, for microscope pictures of Pop Rocks and cotton candy, for proofreading, for going hoarse teaching experiments at USASEF, and for answering many, many strange science questions.

Photos by Loralee Leavitt, Laramie Leavitt, Kent Bassett, and Eliza Grant

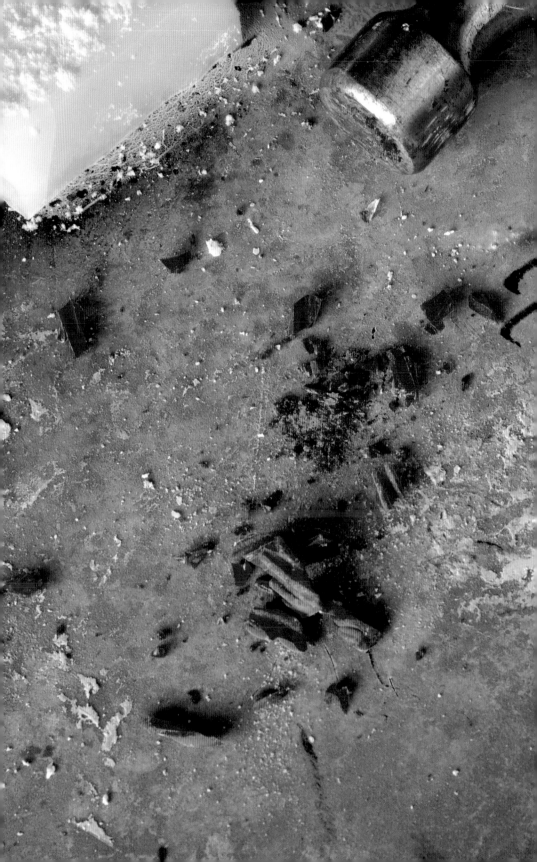

INTRODUCTION

You may think that candy is just a sugary snack. Think again.

With candy, you can explore chemistry with color-changing gummi bears, or dissolve eggshells with acid. Make instant crystals, or break up crystals to turn chocolate into sawdust.

Bend light, or make candy invisible. Turn a piece of candy into an underwater diver, or make Pop Rocks jump like popcorn. Send candy tunneling into ice cubes, or shoot marshmallows out of a bottle.

Just try candy experiments.

EXPERIMENT TIPS

Wear an apron or an old T-shirt, because candy and oil can stain clothes.

Use tap water or room-temperature water unless the instructions say otherwise.

Always ask a grown-up to help you heat candy in the microwave or the oven. Melted candy can get hotter than boiling water. If you touch it, you could get burned.

Never heat a jawbreaker.

Microwave times will depend on what kind of microwave you use. Always watch candy in the microwave to make sure that you don't heat it too much.

When heating candy in the oven, line your baking sheet with foil or parchment paper. This will save you from scrubbing sticky messes!

Keep wet rags or paper towels ready to clean up sticky spills.

Don't eat or drink the experiments. Candy might have germs on it if people have touched and handled it. Baking soda can make you sick if you eat too much.

If you leave candy water sitting around for several days, it might grow mold. If this happens, throw the experiment away and start over.

CANDY EXPERIMENT SCIENCE FAIR PROJECTS

Splash, fizz, bam! Soda spouts all over the school cafeteria as you make a candy soda geyser. What a great science fair project, right?

Actually, no.

A good science fair project is more than just a fun demonstration. For many science fairs, students are asked to use the scientific method to ask and answer a question by doing experiments. This means coming up with a question, doing background research, making a prediction (hypothesis), experimenting, and using your results to answer your question.

SCIENCE DEMONSTRATION:

Mix candy and soda to make a geyser.

SCIENCE FAIR PROJECT:

Research what kind of candy makes the best soda geyser.

Candy experiments make great science fair projects when you use them to ask and answer a question about a scientific principle. Find something that you can test by changing just one experiment variable at a time. For example, instead of combining different candies with different sodas to make geysers, you might test several kinds of candy with one brand of soda to see which kind of candy works best. Then use your research and results to try to explain why this is so. In the candy and soda example, you might explain how a candy's density and surface texture help make soda bubble.

One way to decide whether you've chosen a good question is to ask yourself what kind of chart or graph you can make about your project. If you have answers that you can compare in a chart or graph, you have data that are answering a question.

After you've done your research, make a poster to explain your experiment (preferably on tri-fold poster board because you can stand it up on a table). Include all of these components:

- an introduction explaining your question and why it is important
- a list of materials
- a description of how you did the experiment
- your results, perhaps displayed in a chart or graph
- conclusion, in which you say what you learned

One science fair judge warns that sometimes children spend far more time making a fancy poster than they spend doing the project. Don't spend more time on the fonts than the research!

For more information on creating a good science fair project, see the Science Buddies website at www.sciencebuddies.org/science-fair-projects/project_guide_index.shtml.

Experiments with Science Fair Ideas

- Can You Taste pH?
- Acid Attack
- How Fast Does It Dissolve?
- Candy Ice Tunnels
- Saltwater Gummi Soak
- Soda Geyser Showdown
- Marshmallow Bottle Launcher
- Do Mint and Orange Mix?

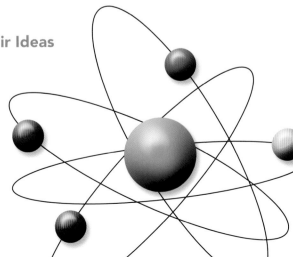

Water is made of hydrogen and oxygen. Sometimes water breaks into smaller pieces of hydrogen (H+) and oxygen/hydrogen (OH–). Both H+ and OH– react with other molecules. But in a glass of pure water, when you have equal amounts of H+ and OH–, you don't see this effect.

An acidic solution contains more H+. Acid reacts with certain kinds of substances, such as baking soda and eggshells. It also creates a sour sensation when you taste it. (Anything that tastes sour contains acid.)

A basic solution contains more OH–. Bases also react with certain kinds of substances, including acids.

In this chapter, you'll use color-changing gummi bears, fizzing candy, and eggs with Warheads to learn about acids and bases.

Photo (right): Warheads Sour Spray is even more acidic than Warheads candy. When you spray it onto an eggshell, it eventually makes the eggshell bubble.

1

ACIDS AND BASES

COLOR-CHANGING GUMMIES

TIME Several hours

SKILL LEVEL Easy

Can you turn a red gummi bear blue?

What you need:

Red gummi bear or gummi worm from a package of Black Forest "Made with Real Fruit Juice" gummi candy

Small clear bowl with ½ cup of water

Baking soda

What to do:

1. Add ½ teaspoon of baking soda to the bowl of water. (Proportions do not need to be exact.)

2. Place the gummi bear in the water.

3. Wait several hours. Do you see a blue rim forming around the edge of the gummi bear?

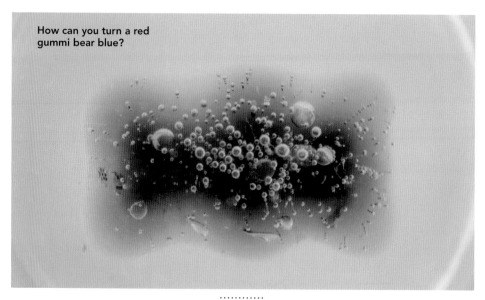

How can you turn a red gummi bear blue?

What's happening:

Black Forest "Made with Real Fruit Juice" gummi bears are colored with natural food extracts, not the petroleum-based dyes used in most candy. The red gummi bears are colored with black carrot extract, which happens to be an acid–base indicator. When it's mixed with a base, it turns blue. So if your black carrot gummi bear absorbs baking soda water, which is basic, it turns blue from the outside in. After two days, it should be completely blue.

Do you notice any bubbles on the gummi bear? These bubbles are created when the baking soda in the water reacts with the citric acid flavoring in the gummi bear. Your gummi bear might end up looking as if it has blisters!

Can you change it back? To try, dump out the baking soda water and put the gummi bear in an acidic solution, like vinegar. (Careful—a water-logged gummi bear is fragile!) Alternatively, you can add acid (such as vinegar) to neutralize the baking soda and turn the water acidic. If the dye hasn't dissolved out of the bear, and if the bear can absorb any more liquid, you might be able to change the color again.

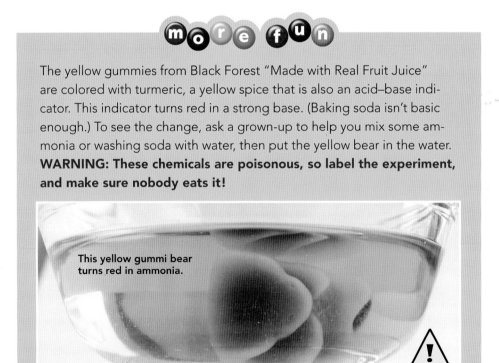

more fun

The yellow gummies from Black Forest "Made with Real Fruit Juice" are colored with turmeric, a yellow spice that is also an acid–base indicator. This indicator turns red in a strong base. (Baking soda isn't basic enough.) To see the change, ask a grown-up to help you mix some ammonia or washing soda with water, then put the yellow bear in the water. **WARNING: These chemicals are poisonous, so label the experiment, and make sure nobody eats it!**

This yellow gummi bear turns red in ammonia.

CAN YOU TASTE PH?

TIME
Up to an hour

SKILL LEVEL
Medium

What can you use to test acidity: pH paper or your tongue? Or both?

What you need:

A variety of sour candies such as Warheads, Lemonheads, Sour Patch Kids, or Skittles

Small bowls

pH indicator paper, ranging from a pH of about 1 to 7 (available on Amazon)

Warm water

What to do:

1. Put a few pieces of candy in each bowl. (Use a separate bowl for each kind of candy.)

2. Pour warm water into each bowl until the candy is covered.

3. Let the sour part of the candy dissolve. (Some candies have a sour shell, and some need to dissolve completely.)

4. Taste a spoonful of water from each bowl. How sour is it?

5. Line the bowls up in order of sourness.

6. Test each bowl of water with a pH indicator strip. Do the results match the results of your tasting?

What's happening:

Sour taste is caused by acid, so the more sour your candy is, the more acid it contains. You should be able to test this both with pH paper and with your tongue.

If your taste test doesn't exactly match the pH paper test, there are a few possible explanations. Sometimes it's hard to tell exactly what result the pH indicator paper gives, especially when you're using it to test colored candy. Also, some flavors might cover up or distract you from acidic tastes.

Can you test sourness?

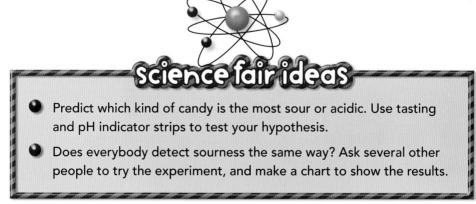

- Predict which kind of candy is the most sour or acidic. Use tasting and pH indicator strips to test your hypothesis.

- Does everybody detect sourness the same way? Ask several other people to try the experiment, and make a chart to show the results.

FIZZING SODA CANDY

TIME 5 minutes

SKILL LEVEL Easy

Does Soda Can Fizzy Candy really fizz like soda pop?

What you need:
Soda Can Fizzy Candy

Clear bowl of water

What to do:
1. Put some candy into the bowl of water. What happens?

What's happening:
Soda Can Fizzy Candy fizzes, but not like soda pop. This kind of candy doesn't contain carbon dioxide bubbles. On the label you'll see what really makes the bubbles: citric acid and sodium bicarbonate (baking soda). When these ingredients get wet and mix together, the reaction creates carbon dioxide bubbles, just like when you mix vinegar and baking soda.

Pop Rocks are actually closer to soda, because they contain carbon dioxide bubbles trapped in the candy. In fact, Pop Rocks were originally invented by a chemist who trapped carbon dioxide in candy tablets because he was trying to create a way for customers to stir up instant sodas. Although the soda idea didn't work, Pop Rocks became a popular candy.

Does Soda Can Fizzy Candy really fizz like soda pop?

m o r e f u n

After you put the Soda Can Fizzy Candy in the water, use the handle of a table knife to crush it into smaller pieces. Do you see more bubbles? Do the bubbles help the tiny pieces float?

ACID DISSOLVING TEST

TIME 1 hour

SKILL LEVEL Medium

**Your digestive system uses acid.
Does that mean that acid dissolves candy?**

What you need:

Candy that dissolves easily,
such as conversation hearts,
Skittles, Jolly Ranchers, or Nerds

Small clear bowls

Room-temperature water

Vinegar

What to do:

1. Pour vinegar in one bowl and water in another bowl. (If you have several kinds of candy, you may want to pour more bowls.)

2. Put one piece of candy in vinegar and one in water.

3. Check your candy every few minutes. Which dissolves faster?

What's happening:

You might think that since your stomach contains acid, the acetic acid in vinegar will break up or dissolve candy. But acetic acid reacts only with certain kinds of substances—and sugar isn't one of them. In fact, candy might dissolve more slowly in vinegar, since the acetic acid molecules don't dissolve sugar as well as water does.

Although your stomach does contain acid, it plays less of a role in digestion than you might think. Acids don't break up components in your food like carbohydrates (such as sugar) or fats. That work is done by digestive enzymes (although some of those reactions go faster when acid is present).

Does candy dissolve faster in water or vinegar?

ACID ATTACK

TIME
1 week

SKILL LEVEL
Advanced

**Warheads are sour because they contain acid.
What can this acid react with?**

What you need:

10 to 20 Warheads

Small clear bowl with ½ cup of water

Whole egg or broken eggshell

What to do:

1. Add 10 Warheads to the bowl of water. Wait a few minutes, stirring occasionally.

2. When the white coating on the Warheads has dissolved completely, use a spoon to take the Warheads out of the bowl. (The white coating contains most of the acid, so dissolving the rest of the candy won't make the water more acidic.)

3. Put the egg in the water. Check back every few hours. Do you see bubbles?

4. If you have extra Warheads, replace the water after the first day. Mix up a new bowl of Warhead water, following the above steps. Remove the egg from the old bowl, wipe off the bubbles, and put it in the new bowl. Discard the water from the old bowl.

5. Check the egg every day for up to a week, then remove it from the bowl. How does it feel? How does it look?

Two weeks in
Warheads solution
made this eggshell
start to dissolve.

What's happening:

An eggshell contains calcium carbonate. (That's what makes it hard.) When you put the egg in the Warheads solution, the acid splits up the calcium carbonate. The calcium dissolves into the water, and the carbonate reacts with the acid to make carbon dioxide. This makes bubbles form on the outside of the eggshell.

Cavities are formed by a similar reaction. Tooth enamel is made of calcium phosphate, which like the calcium carbonate in eggshells reacts with acid. Tooth enamel contains more calcium than eggshells, and it dissolves in a different pattern, so teeth are more protected than eggs. But acid can still soften or weaken tooth enamel. Citric acid, often found in candy and soda, is especially bad for teeth.

Does this mean that if you eat 10 Warheads, your teeth will dissolve? Not necessarily. Your mouth protects itself against cavities in ways that an egg can't. When you're eating or drinking something, you usually swallow it instead of holding it in your mouth. Your saliva can wash away, or dilute, leftover acids. Saliva also adds minerals to your teeth, rebuilding some of the enamel that acid has attacked. You can also protect your teeth after eating something sour by drinking water to dilute the acid, then brushing your teeth immediately.

Acid from food and soda can cause tooth decay. But regular cavities, caused when food or sugar sticks in teeth and gets turned to acid by bacteria, are still a bigger problem. The best way to protect your teeth? Eat sugar less frequently.

What can these Warheads do to this tooth?

Alternative:

If you've lost a tooth recently, or if your parents have saved any of your baby teeth, do this experiment with a tooth instead of an eggshell. Check it every day. Does the tooth change color or get softer? If your tooth eventually vanishes, don't be surprised—the acids in a Warhead can dissolve a tooth entirely!

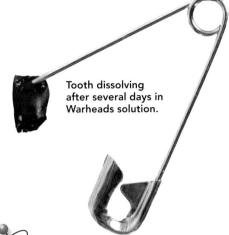

Tooth dissolving after several days in Warheads solution.

science fair ideas

● Any acid will dissolve eggshell (although if it's not a strong acid, the results might be hard to see). What happens when you try this with vinegar, lemon juice, or other acids? Can you predict which acid will dissolve the most eggshell? What if you try this experiment with teeth?

● Fluoride helps protect teeth against acid erosion. You can see this for yourself with the "Crest Eggsperiment." Rub fluoride toothpaste onto the top half of an eggshell, rub it off after a few hours, label the top with marker, and put the egg in acid. What happens to the different parts of the eggshell? Find the complete experiment at www.crest.com/crest-kids/eggsperiment.aspx.

When you drop candy in water, a magical dance begins. The water molecules bump into the sugar molecules, knocking them away from the solid candy to float around in the water. The solid candy appears to shrink as its molecules strip off and float away. The candy is dissolving.

In this chapter, you'll use dissolving races to see what makes candy dissolve faster. You'll try dissolving candy in different types of liquid. You'll make dissolving candy dig tunnels through ice cubes. And you'll find candy that only partly dissolves, leaving surprising results. Let the dissolving races begin!

2
DISSOLVE

STIRRING RACE

Can stirring make sugar dissolve faster?

What you need:

Pixy Stix (or salt or sugar)

Two clear glasses filled with equal amounts of water

Spoon or stirring stick

What to do:

1. Pour an equal amount of Pixy Stix into each glass of water.

2. Stir one glass. Does the candy dissolve faster?

What's happening:

When sugar dissolves, the loose sugar molecules float around in the water. But when these molecules bump into solid sugar crystals, they can latch onto the crystals and re-form into solids. So if you have a pile of sugar sitting at the bottom of a glass, the dissolving sugars keep re-forming into solids, and the total amount of sugar is slow to dissolve completely.

When you stir the solution, the dissolved sugar molecules are carried away from the sugar crystals and separated. Without solid crystals to latch onto, or other floating sugar molecules to join together to make crystals, the dissolved sugar stays dissolved. More of the solid sugar dissolves into the water, until at last the solid particles are gone.

VOCABULARY:

Solute: stuff that dissolves

Solvent: the liquid in which the solute dissolves

Stirring helps Pixy Stix dissolve faster.

more fun

As you stir the Pixy Stix into the water, drag the spoon back and forth across the bottom of the glass and watch for colored swirls. You might make tiny Pixy Stix tornadoes!

Try this experiment with Pop Rocks. Since the Pop Rocks release bubbles when they dissolve, you'll be able to hear which dissolves faster.

HOW MUCH DISSOLVES?

TIME
10 minutes

SKILL LEVEL
Get a grown-up

If you put too much candy in a bowl of water, some of it won't dissolve. How can you dissolve all of the candy?

What you need:

Candy that dissolves easily, such as Pixy Stix, Nerds, or smashed Jolly Ranchers (alternative: sugar)

Microwave-safe bowl with about ½ cup of cold water

Microwave

What to do:

1. Add a large spoonful of candy or sugar to the bowl of water and stir. Does all of the candy dissolve? (If it does, add more.)

2. Heat the bowl in the microwave. Stir again. Does more of the candy dissolve?

More Pixy Stix powder dissolves in hot water than in ice water.

What's happening:

A kid with a lot of energy wants to run, jump, or play—not sit down. Molecules act the same way. A molecule with a lot of energy vibrates, changes shape, and moves around a lot. It doesn't easily lock into place with other solid molecules.

When you dissolve sugar in cold water, the sugar molecules break away from their solid crystal lattice and mix into the water. But some of the dissolved sugars bump into sugar crystals, latch back on, and become solid again. When this dissolving and recrystallizing happens at the same rate, the water can't dissolve any more sugar than it already has. The water is saturated.

When you heat the water up, the water molecules move faster. They hit the sugar molecules with more energy, knocking them loose into the water. The sugar molecules, also moving faster, don't latch onto crystals as easily. Instead of re-forming crystals, they stay dissolved.

This allows more sugar molecules to mix into the water. The more you heat the water, the more sugar can dissolve. In fact, one cup of boiling water can dissolve two cups of sugar (the recipe for rock candy).

VOCABULARY

Saturated: a solution that has dissolved as much solute as it can. No more solute can dissolve.

Once the solution has cooled down, does the dissolved candy or sugar recrystallize into solid form?

If you spoon too much sugar into a bowl of cold water, sugar keeps dissolving even after the solution is saturated. How can that be? Because as some sugar dissolves into the water, other sugar crystallizes back into solid form to create new grains of sugar at the bottom of the cup. You'll always have the same amount of sugar—but it won't always be the same sugar!

HOW FAST DOES IT DISSOLVE?

TIME 10 minutes

SKILL LEVEL Easy

**Sugar dissolves in water.
What happens if that water already has sugar in it?**

What you need:

Candy with a shell that dissolves quickly, such as Skittles, Nerds, or chewy Lemonheads

Clear small bowls

Water

Sugary liquids, such as fruit juice, Gatorade, soda, syrup, or corn syrup

Sugar (optional)

What to do:

1. Pour water into one bowl. Fill another bowl with each type of sugary liquid.

2. Put an equal number of candies in each bowl or cup. How fast do they dissolve?

Alternative:

Take three bowls and pour a cup of water into each. Add ¼ cup of sugar to one bowl and ½ cup of sugar to another bowl. Put a piece of candy in each bowl, and see which dissolves fastest.

What's happening:

A liquid (or solvent) can only dissolve a certain amount of stuff (solute). If a liquid already has some sugar dissolved in it, the new candy will dissolve less quickly. Once the liquid has dissolved all the sugar it can, it is "saturated," and nothing else will dissolve in it (unless you heat it up or make some other change). When you put candy into a sugary liquid, it will dissolve more slowly than in pure water.

Does the candy in soda dissolve more quickly than you expect? The carbonation, or bubbles, might be stirring up the soda. When the liquid is stirred, it can dissolve more sugar. To have a head-to-head competition between soda and juice, you need to stir the soda or let it sit out to get rid of the bubbles.

Why is fruit juice on this list of sugary liquids? Because fruit juice can contain a lot of sugar. In fact, some juices are more sugary than soda pop (perhaps because the soda pop is matching the sweetness we like in juice). Because of the sugar, doctors now advise children not to drink too much juice. Juice makes a fun treat, but if you're really thirsty, try water instead.

Why do Skittles dissolve faster in water than in white grape juice?

science fair ideas

● Test the sugar concentration of different liquids by seeing how long it takes to dissolve equal amounts of candy or sugar in each one. Compare results. Does the candy in the most sugary liquid dissolve the slowest? If not, what else might be affecting your experiment?

THE GHOST LOLLIPOP

TIME 5 minutes

SKILL LEVEL Easy

When you put a swirl lollipop in water, where does the color go?

What you need:

Swirl lollipop made of coiled candy

Clear dish filled with 1 to 2 inches of water

What to do:

1. Lay down the lollipop in the bowl so that it is half in and half out of the water, with the stick leaning against the side of the dish.

2. Wait several minutes. What happens to the color?

What's happening:

On this kind of lollipop, the color is only on the outside. Dissolve away the color, and you turn the lollipop into a ghostly imitation of its former self.

Half-dissolved lollipop.

HALF-AND-HALF PEEPS

TIME 10 minutes

SKILL LEVEL Easy

Can you turn your Peeps into painted sports fans?

What you need:

Peeps candy

Clear bowl of water

What to do:

1. Place a Peep into the bowl of water and let it float.

2. Check back every few minutes. How does the candy look?

What's happening:

Marshmallows don't dissolve in water, but sugar does. When you let Peeps candy float, the colored sugar on the submerged part of the candy dissolves, leaving white behind.

Half-and-half Peeps.

DOES A GUMMI WORM DISSOLVE?

TIME 2 days

SKILL LEVEL Easy

A gummi worm can absorb so much water that it doubles in length. What else changes?

What you need:

Gummi worm or other gummi candy

Clear dish filled with a few inches of water

What to do:

1 Put the gummi worm into the dish of water.

2 Wait 2 days. Look at the water—has it taken on a colored tint?

What's happening:

Gelatin doesn't dissolve quickly in water. But the other ingredients, like the sugar and the dye, can dissolve. If you put a gummi candy in water and then let it absorb water, it looks like a gelatin dessert. But because the flavor and sugar have dissolved, it wouldn't taste like one!

There's another reason not to eat a watery gummi worm. Once you add water to something, it's more likely that bacteria will grow there. In fact, gelatin is sometimes used in science projects for culturing bacteria (letting bacteria grow so that they can be studied). The bacteria make the gummi worm unsafe to eat. If you leave your gummi worm out long enough, you might even see mold start to grow. Yuck!

Will this gummi worm dissolve?

VANISHING COTTON CANDY

Can you make cotton candy vanish instantly?

What you need:

Cotton candy

Clear bowl of water

What to do:

1 Drop a puff of cotton candy into the bowl of water. What happens?

What's happening:

Cotton candy is made from melted sugar spun into fine strands. When you put it in water, it dissolves.

Why does this happen so quickly? The sugar is spun into tiny thin strands, so there is more surface area. Because so much of the sugar is exposed to the water, cotton candy can dissolve far more quickly than other kinds of candy.

Cotton candy dissolves
almost instantly.

more fun

Add a teaspoon of baking soda to the bowl of water, and drop in some
sour cotton candy (often available at Halloween). Does the acidic candy
react with the baking soda to make bubbles?

THE COTTON CANDY SPONGE

When you put cotton candy in water, it dissolves immediately. What happens when you put it in oil?

What you need:

Cotton candy

Small bowl with about ½ inch of cooking oil, such as vegetable or olive oil

What to do:

1. Dip the cotton candy into the oil at the bottom of the bowl. What happens?

2. Let the cotton candy sit in the oil. How much oil can it soak up?

What's happening:

When you dip cotton candy in water, it dissolves so fast it seems to disappear. But sugar doesn't dissolve in oil. When you dip cotton candy in oil, it soaks up oil like a sponge.

Why does cotton candy soak up anything at all? Because of capillary action. The molecules in the oil are attracted to the sugar molecules in the cotton candy. When the fibers of the cotton candy are close together, this attraction is strong enough for the oil to seep upward into the candy (even when gravity is pulling the other way). How fast it rises depends on the surface tension of the liquid and how far apart the fibers are.

Remember not to pour used oil down the drain! To dispose of oil, place it in a container and throw it away, or donate it to a site that collects cooking oil.

Instead of dissolving in oil,
cotton candy soaks it up.

more fun

If you let your cotton candy absorb just the right amount of oil, it can
start to feel brittle and crispy. This may be because the oil replaces any
water that softens the candy.

CANDY ICE TUNNELS

TIME 30 minutes

SKILL LEVEL Easy

When you put these candies on ice, they dig right in!

What you need:

Candy that dissolves easily, such as Skittles, Jolly Ranchers, jawbreakers, or conversation hearts

Ice (preferably in an ice cube tray so that it doesn't slide or tip)

What to do:

1. Put the ice cube tray on a flat surface, or put an ice cube on a plate.

2. Place a piece of candy on each ice cube. (Make sure it will not slide off.)

3. Wait 10 to 20 minutes. Does the candy sink into the ice?

What's happening:

As the sugar dissolves off of the candy, it mixes with the liquid water from the melting ice cube. Sugar water has a lower freezing point than regular water, so the sugar water melts the ice beneath it.

more fun

Because sugar lowers the melting point of ice, you can use candy to melt ice cubes that are still in the freezer. Put some Skittles on ice cubes in your freezer and check back in a few hours. Do they seem to dig into the ice?

Skittles candy
tunneling into ice.

science fair ideas

- Sugar isn't the only substance that lowers the freezing point of ice. Salt also does this, which is why salt is spread on roads for ice removal in winter weather. What other substances can you test on ice? Which melts ice the fastest? Can you do some research to find out why?

When something melts, it is softened by heat until it turns into a liquid. Melting helps you soften chocolate, liquefy conversation hearts, and turn gummi candy into something surprisingly familiar.

Melting is sometimes confused with dissolving, because in both cases, a solid can become liquid. But they are different processes. When candy melts, heat makes the sugar molecules vibrate faster and faster, softening the candy. When candy dissolves, the solid candy loses molecules that float away in water. Of course, some experiments involve both melting and dissolving, such as making a puddle of Peeps.

Think boiling water is hot? Melted candy can be much hotter. To be safe, always have a grown-up help you heat candy in the microwave or the oven. Watch the candy as it melts. If it starts looking burned, or starts to smoke, turn off the heat. Use hot pads to pick up hot plates or pans. Never touch hot candy with your bare fingers. Instead, test how soft it is by poking it with a fork.

3

MELT

"CHOCOLATE" CONVERSATION HEARTS

TIME
30 minutes

SKILL LEVEL
Get a grown-up

Can you transform sugary hearts into chocolate puddles?

What you need:

Conversation hearts

Baking sheet lined with aluminum foil or parchment paper

Oven

What to do:

1. Preheat the oven to 400°F.

2. Place the conversation hearts on the baking sheet and put them in the oven.

3. Check every few minutes. Do the hearts start to melt? Do they turn shiny? Do they brown until they look like melted chocolate? **(CAUTION—they're too hot to touch!)**

What's happening:

Conversation hearts are made from dextrose, corn syrup, and table sugar (sucrose). When they are heated, the sugars start to brown. Eventually the melted sugar darkens so much that it looks like melted chocolate. If you heat it long enough, it will blacken.

Even though you don't see flames, the sugars are actually oxidizing (burning) a little bit. Sugar molecules are made from carbon, oxygen, and hydrogen atoms. When sugar burns, the hydrogen and oxygen are stripped away, combining with molecules in the air to form water and carbon dioxide, leaving behind black carbon ash. When sugar only partially burns, many of the molecules are changed in small ways. The resulting molecules form the various compounds that make up caramel.

Chocolate conversation hearts?

PUDDLE O' PEEPS

TIME 5 minutes

SKILL LEVEL Get a grown-up

What happens when you give Peeps candy a hot bath?

What you need:

Peeps candy or large marshmallow

Large microwave-safe clear bowl

Water

Microwave

What to do:

1. Ask a grown-up to boil some water and pour it into the bowl, filling the bowl at least halfway.
(Alternative: Ask a grown-up to microwave a bowlful of water until it boils.)
(CAUTION—boiling water can burn you!)

2. Put the Peeps candy in the bowl and watch it melt into a puddle. Look underneath it—do you see air bubbles?

What's happening:

The gelatin in marshmallows doesn't dissolve in cold water, but it melts when it's hot. This is why marshmallows melt so nicely in hot chocolate.

As the marshmallow melts, the trapped air bubbles expand. This is why you see so many bubbles in your puddle o' Peeps.

Peeps melting into a puddle.

GULPING GUMMIES

Is this liquid-filled gummi erupting? Or just melting?

What you need:

Liquid-filled gummi candy, such as Starburst GummiBursts

Microwave-safe plate or piece of parchment paper

Microwave

What to do:

1. Place the candy on the plate or paper.

2. Microwave on medium heat until the filling starts to bubble out.

What's happening:

If the liquid filling in a piece of candy contains water, microwaving it will turn some of the water to steam. The steaming liquid melts through the side or top of the candy to escape, which can make the candy look like it's erupting or gulping.

Why doesn't the liquid filling dissolve the candy from the inside out? Perhaps the thick, sugary liquid is so saturated that it can't dissolve anything else.

Gummi candy erupting as it melts.

Microwave a piece of Twizzlers Filled Twists candy. The steaming, bubbling filling makes the candy look like a heaving, breathing snake!

GUMMI WORM JELL-O

TIME 5 minutes

SKILL LEVEL Get a grown-up

Can you turn a gummi worm into a cafeteria dessert?

What you need:

Gummi worm

Small microwave-safe bowl

Microwave

Water

Half gummi worm, half cafeteria dessert.

What to do:

1. Put the gummi worm in the bowl.

2. Add enough water to barely cover the gummi worm (about 2 tablespoons).

3. Microwave until hot, and stir occasionally. The gummi worm should melt and dissolve completely.

4. Place in the refrigerator. After a few hours, what does it look like?

What's happening:

Gummi candy is mostly sugar, water, color, and gelatin. So are gelatin desserts—they just have more water. If you dissolve a gummi worm and cool it down, it turns into something like your standard cafeteria dessert: Jell-O.

Some kinds of candy have a secret ingredient: water. Other kinds of candy change when they get wet. You can see the effects if you just add (or remove) water.

4

JUST ADD (OR REMOVE) WATER

WORMY COTTON CANDY

TIME 5 minutes

SKILL LEVEL Easy

Are invisible worms eating this cotton candy?

What you need:

Cotton candy (the fresh-spun kind may work better than the bagged supermarket variety)

Water

Eyedropper or syringe (optional)

What to do:

1. Dip your finger in water, or fill the eyedropper with water.

2. Drop a single water droplet onto the cotton candy.

3. Watch the water spread out as it dissolves the cotton candy. Does the water look as if it's eating the cotton candy?

What's happening:

When cotton candy gets wet, the sugar dissolves. But each tiny droplet of water can dissolve only a little bit of sugar. The water travels along the fibers of the cotton candy, dissolving sugar as it goes. This makes the cotton candy look like it's being eaten by invisible worms.

At some point, each droplet of water becomes saturated. (It has absorbed all the sugar it can.) The water droplet stops moving. Touch one—does it feel sticky? That's because it is full of sticky dissolved sugar.

Water drops "eat" this cotton candy.

EASTER GRASS SPAGHETTI

TIME
10 minutes

SKILL LEVEL
Easy

Can you make "spaghetti" out of Edible Easter Grass?

What you need:

Edible Easter Grass candy

Clear glass of water

What to do:

1 Put the Easter Grass into the glass of water.

2 After a few minutes, stir the Easter Grass with a spoon. Has it softened?

What's happening:

Easter Grass is made from potato and corn starches, long stiff chains of sugar molecules that have bonded together. (Sugar molecules don't taste sweet when they're chained together to make starch.) In turn, these long, stiff molecules are bonded to each other, making rigid strands of Easter Grass.

When you put the Easter Grass in water, the starch soaks up water like a sponge. As it does, the water breaks the bonds between the starch molecules. The water also slips between starch molecules, allowing them to slide past each other. This makes the Easter Grass more pliable (bendable).

Dip strands of Easter Grass in water, then pull them out and arrange them on a piece of paper to make designs. The sticky wet Easter Grass will stick to the paper.

Water turns this Edible Easter Grass into spaghetti.

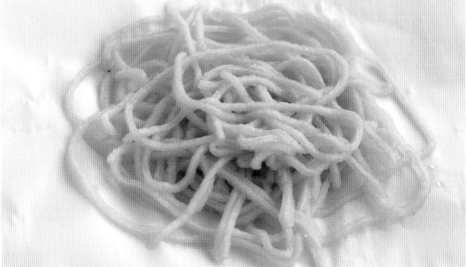

SEIZE CHOCOLATE

TIME 10 minutes

SKILL LEVEL Get a grown-up

For a candy maker, what's worse than a candy thief?
Chocolate that gets "seized"!

What you need:

Solid chocolate candy, such as a chocolate bar

Microwave-safe bowl

Microwave

Water

Spoon for stirring

What to do:

1. Put the chocolate in the bowl.

2. Microwave on low heat to melt the chocolate. Try stirring it every 30 seconds to see if it has started to melt. (You can't always tell whether the chocolate has melted just by looking.) Don't overheat the chocolate, or it will turn thick and lumpy.

3. When the chocolate has melted, stir it together.

4. Add a few drops of water and keep stirring. What happens? (If nothing happens, add a little more water and try again.)

What's happening:

There are a few reasons that chocolate and water don't mix well. Chocolate contains cocoa butter, a type of fat. Fats don't mix easily with water. But something else in the chocolate does mix with water: sugar. When water is added to the chocolate, it starts to dissolve the sugar. The sugar clumps together, forming a sticky syrup. Suddenly your smooth chocolate mixture of cocoa butter, cocoa solids, and sugar starts to separate, as the sugars stick to the cocoa solids, excluding the cocoa butter. The result can be a lumpy, grainy mess.

Candy makers say that when water mixes with chocolate, it "seizes." Once chocolate has seized, it can no longer be used to make chocolate candies.

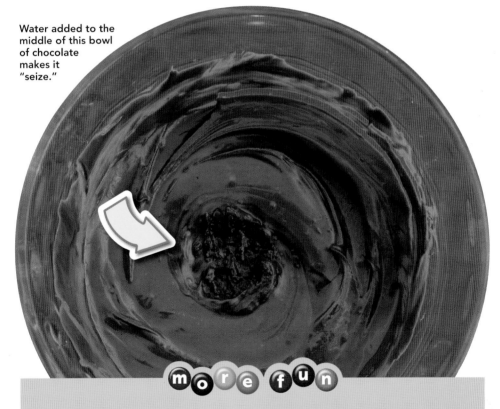

Water added to the middle of this bowl of chocolate makes it "seize."

more fun

Once you've made your chocolate seize, can you turn it back into a smooth paste? Try stirring in hot water to melt the cocoa butter, or add small amounts of vegetable oil or shortening to dissolve the cocoa butter. This paste can then be added to a recipe for a chocolate dessert, or mixed into hot milk for hot chocolate.

PALE CHOCOLATE

TIME 10 minutes

SKILL LEVEL Easy

**Chocolate doesn't dissolve in water.
So why does wet chocolate turn pale?**

What you need:

Chocolate

Dish of water

What to do:

1 Put the chocolate in the water.

2 Check back after a few minutes.

What's happening:

You might think that chocolate won't react with cold water. After all, it's made of cocoa butter, a fat, which doesn't dissolve in water. But that's not the only ingredient in chocolate.

Chocolate is made from sugar, cocoa butter (the white fat from cocoa beans), and cocoa powder, the brown cocoa solids from cocoa beans. When chocolate is put in water, the cocoa butter doesn't react. But the cocoa powder does. It absorbs water and expands. This change makes the chocolate paler.

If you take the chocolate out of the water and let it dry, it will return to its regular color.

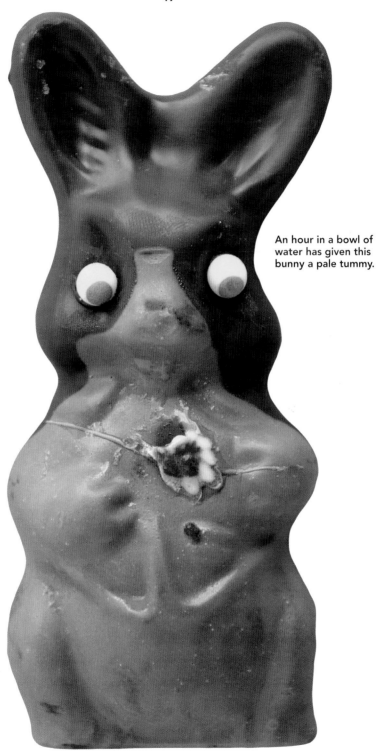

An hour in a bowl of water has given this bunny a pale tummy.

DYEING GUMMI WORMS

TIME
2 days

SKILL
LEVEL
Easy

What you need:

Gummi worms or other gummi candy

Food coloring

Bowl of water

Dish

What to do:

1 Add a few drops of food coloring to the bowl of water.

2 Put the gummi candy in the water, and wait up to 2 days. Did your gummi candy change color?

What's happening:

Because the protein molecules in gelatin entangle water, gummi candy absorbs water and expands. If there's dye in the water, it gets absorbed too, dyeing your gummi worm different colors. What color combinations can you create?

Adding blue dye turns these yellow gummies green.

Turn a red and white gummi worm completely blue, using a Black Forest "Made with Real Fruit Juice" brand gummi worm. Fill a dish with water, add blue food coloring, and add baking soda. As the gummi worm absorbs water, it absorbs the blue food coloring as well. Meanwhile, the red sections of the gummi worm start turning blue as the black carrot extract reacts to the basic baking soda water. Eventually the whole gummi worm turns blue.

Blue dye and a little bit of chemistry turn these gummies completely blue.

SALTWATER GUMMI SOAK

TIME
2 days

SKILL LEVEL
Medium

What you need:

4 gummi worms or other gummi candy

3 small clear bowls with about 1 cup of water each

Sugar

Salt

What to do:

1. Add a spoonful of sugar to one bowl of water, and a spoonful of salt to another bowl of water.

2. Put a gummi candy in each bowl, and set the extra gummi bear aside for comparison.

   After several hours, check the gummi candies to see what size they are. Which ones have changed the most?

What's happening:

A cup of fresh water is a dilute solution. When you put salt in water, you make a concentrated solution. The more salt, the more concentrated the solution is. If water can pass from a dilute solution into a concentrated one, it will. Nature is trying to make the two solutions equally concentrated. This process is called osmosis.

You can see osmosis in action when you put a gummi worm in fresh water. Water flows into the gummi worm, diluting the sugary gelatin mix (a concentrated solution). The gummi worm expands. But if you put a gummi worm in salt water, the salt water is already concentrated. Not as much water is needed to dilute the gummi worm, so the gummi worm will expand less. In fact, depending on how concentrated your solution is, it might not expand at all.

Osmosis is also the process that draws water into plant roots and up where it's needed. If you watered plants with salt water, the plant cells wouldn't be able to absorb any water, just like gummi bears.

Which gummi worm is
sitting in salt water?

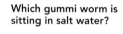

science fair ideas

- Mix up different solutions with different substances and put a
  gummi bear in each. Predict which gummi bear will expand the
  most and which will expand the least.

SHATTER PEEPS

TIME 1 hour

SKILL LEVEL Get a grown-up

Water helps make marshmallows stretchy and elastic. What happens if you remove the water?

What you need:

Peeps marshmallow candy or other marshmallows

Baking sheet lined with aluminum foil or parchment paper

Oven

What to do:

1. Heat the oven to 250°F.

2. Place a marshmallow on the baking sheet and put it in the oven.

3. Check the marshmallow every 10 minutes. Remove it after about an hour and let it cool. What does it feel like?

What's happening:

Marshmallows are made of sugar, gelatin, and water. When you heat one in a microwave, or on high heat, the water turns to steam and puffs up the marshmallow. But if you heat it in an oven on low heat, you can evaporate the water without destroying the marshmallow.

After your marshmallow cools down, it should be hard and brittle. Then it's easy to break.

A Peeps marshmallow shatters after time in the oven.

more fun

When you break a brittle marshmallow, listen closely. You might hear a crackling sound.

CAN YOU FRY A CADBURY EGG?

TIME 30 minutes

SKILL LEVEL Get a grown-up

A Cadbury Egg looks like a real egg. Can you cook it?

What you need:

Cadbury Easter egg

Baking sheet lined with foil or parchment paper

Oven

Spoon

Frying pan and stove (alternative)

What to do:

1. Preheat your oven to about 300°F.

2. Crack open the Cadbury egg. Use a spoon to scoop the filling out onto the baking sheet.

3. Heat the egg in the oven for 10 to 20 minutes. Check back every few minutes. What's happening?

Alternative:

Heat the frying pan to medium on the stovetop, then scoop the filling into the pan. Watch as it bubbles like a real egg. After a few minutes, turn the heat off and let the pan cool. (You may want to clean the pan before the candy cools completely, because it's softer and easier to scrape off.)

What's happening:

Like most soft candy, the filling of a Cadbury egg contains an unlisted ingredient: water. The water determines whether a candy will be liquid, runny, soft, or hard.

When you heat the Cadbury Egg filling, some of the water evaporates, leaving sugar, dye, and other ingredients. The sugars melt together, making the "egg" look cooked.

Of course, cooking a Cadbury Egg isn't really like cooking an egg. A real egg contains protein. When the egg is heated, the protein molecules move faster, causing them to uncoil from spring-like shapes into long strands. Then the protein molecules start joining together to form a solid, water-trapping mass. This makes the egg white look opaque. When you "cook" a Cadbury egg, the filling starts out opaque but turns translucent if you heat it enough to melt the sugars.

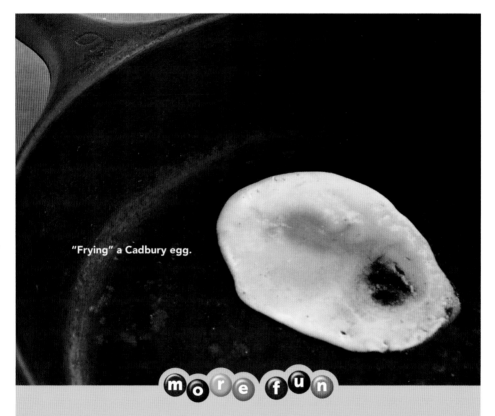

"Frying" a Cadbury egg.

Most soft candy will harden if you heat it enough. Try this with taffy, Starbursts, Tootsie Rolls, or other soft, chewy candies.

even more fun

Put a Cadbury egg in the freezer, then cut it in half. The colder filling should have hardened slightly. If it's cold enough, it can even feel hard-boiled!

A puff of cotton candy dissolves on the tongue to nearly nothing. Why? Because it isn't very dense. Even though it looks huge, there's hardly any sugar there.

Density is a measure of mass (how much something weighs) divided by volume (how big it is). A puff of cotton candy is not very dense—until you roll it into the tightest ball possible.

Density makes cotton candy light like a cloud, instead of heavy like a rock. Density makes Tootsie Rolls sink, and density makes them rise again. Density keeps Pop Rocks swimming when they bubble, and density keeps them from sinking through thick sugary liquid.

Get ready to make candy shrink, sink, and float. You just have to change the density.

5

DENSITY

SHRINK COTTON CANDY

TIME
5 minutes

SKILL LEVEL
Easy

A huge roll of cotton candy is the biggest dessert you can eat—right?

What you need:

Cotton candy

What to do:

1. Roll the cotton candy into a ball. How small can you smash it?

What's happening:

Cotton candy, like a cotton ball, is made of a collection of tiny threads. These threads are spun from pure sugar, which gets melted and blown out through tiny holes to form strands. They are then gathered together to make the cotton candy. No matter what flavor or color it is, cotton candy is mostly air.

When cotton candy is puffy and full of air, it is not very dense. When you compress the same amount of candy into a smaller space, you are making it denser.

How small can you squash
your cotton candy?

more fun

Cotton candy also becomes denser when you melt it in the oven. Put a
puff on a lined baking sheet, and ask a grown-up to help you heat it to
see how flat it gets.

CAN YOU FLOAT A SUNKEN CANDY BAR?

TIME 10 minutes

SKILL LEVEL Medium

Can you make a sunken candy bar swirl to the surface?

What you need:

Small or mini Milky Way or Snickers bar, unwrapped. Make sure it is not cracked or smashed.

Small clear glass with about 1 cup of water

Salt

Measuring cup and spoon

What to do:

1 Put the candy bar into the glass of water. Does it float or sink?

2 Remove the candy bar.

3 Add 3 tablespoons of salt to the glass. Stir until the salt is dissolved.

4 Put the candy bar back into the glass. Now does it float or sink?

What's happening:

When a candy bar is denser than water, it sinks. But when you add salt to the water, you make the water denser. If you make it dense enough, the candy bar floats.

How can you float a sunken
Snickers bar?

more fun

Can you make a Milky Way bar magically swirl to the surface? To find
out, try this. Pour 1 cup of water into the clear glass. Add 2 tablespoons
of salt, and stir until it dissolves. Add the candy bar. Then add another
1 tablespoon of salt, and gently stir the solution. Does your Milky Way
bar float?

SWIMMING GUMMI FROG

TIME 2 days

SKILL LEVEL Easy

Can you make a gummi frog swim?

What you need:

Gummi candy frog with a marshmallow coating on the bottom, such as a Haribo brand frog

Clear dish of water

What to do:

1 Drop the frog into the dish of water.

2 Wait 2 days. What happens to the frog? What can you see in the marshmallow?

What's happening:

As the gummi frog absorbs water, several things start to happen. The frog absorbs water and expands. As it does, its density changes, becoming closer to the water it is absorbing. It also stretches out the marshmallow, expanding the air bubbles. (Look closely, and you can actually see the air bubbles.) It might also be losing heavy sugar, since sugar dissolves into the surrounding water.

As the frog absorbs water, its density (weight and volume) becomes closer to that of the water surrounding it. If the air bubbles underneath get big enough, there's just enough change in density to gently lift the gummi frog off of the bottom of the bowl.

What makes this gummi frog swim?

TOOTSIE RISING

TIME
1 day

SKILL LEVEL
Easy

When you leave an unwrapped Tootsie candy in water, it eventually dissolves into a puddle in the bottom of the glass. Why is a wrapped one different?

What you need:

Tootsie Roll or Tootsie Pop, wrapped

Clear glass or bottle of water

What to do:

1. Drop the wrapped Tootsie candy into the glass of water. Does it sink?

2. Wait about 12 hours. Does the candy float?

What's happening:

Several things combine to propel the Tootsie candy upward. Tootsie candy is denser than water, making the wrapped candy sink. But when it dissolves, the dense sugar water drains out of the package and sinks to the bottom of the glass. If it's replaced with fresh water, it becomes less dense. The waxed paper wrapper is also less dense than water. Meanwhile, the tiny air bubbles contained in a Tootsie candy might get trapped inside the wrapper. Put all these things together, and you end up with a floating candy wrapper.

Why does the pink Tootsie Pop float after 12 hours in water?

SWIMMING POP ROCKS

TIME
15 minutes

SKILL LEVEL
Easy

When do Pop Rocks not sink?
When they're on top of other Pop Rocks.

What you need:

Two packages of Pop Rocks

Narrow glass filled with water

What to do:

1. Pour 1 package of Pop Rocks into the glass of water. Let it dissolve completely. Don't stir!

2. Pour in the second package of Pop Rocks. How far do they sink? Do any of them float?

What's happening:

When you dissolve the first package of Pop Rocks, you make a dense sugar solution at the bottom of the cup. When you pour in the second package, the new Pop Rocks don't all sink into the dense solution. Even better, because the sugar water is so dense, the new Pop Rocks might float when they form bubbles.

Pop Rocks swimming in dense sugar water.

Pick bubbles and see which rise fastest for a Pop Rocks bubble race.

If you used two packages that were the same color, save this glass for
Pop Rocks Density Layers on page 70.

POP ROCKS DENSITY LAYERS

TIME 20 minutes

SKILL LEVEL Medium

If you pour together colored solutions of different densities, you can make density layers. Can you make density layers without pouring?

What you need:

3 packages of Pop Rocks (two packages of one color, one package of a different color)

Narrow glass filled with water (*alternative: use the glass from the Swimming Pop Rocks experiment on page 68, and start at step 2*)

What to do:

1. Pour 2 packages of the same color Pop Rocks into the glass of water. Wait several minutes until the Pop Rocks dissolve.

2. Pour the other package of colored Pop Rocks into the water. Do they mix with the colored water or float on top?

What's happening:

A less-dense liquid will float on top of a denser liquid. (This is why oil floats on water.) When you dissolve the first two packages of Pop Rocks, you create a dense sugar solution at the bottom of the cup. When you add the third package, the Pop Rocks float on top of that dense solution before they dissolve to create a stripe of color.

Pop Rocks dissolve in colored density layers.

Many kinds of candy contain a secret ingredient: air bubbles. When you release the bubbles, you can flip gummi marshmallow candy, make Pop Rocks puff up and bubble, create bubbling soda geysers, and send candy on a dive. Get ready to free the bubbles!

Photo (right): Microscopic bubbles give these Pop Rocks their pop.

6

FREE THE BUBBLES

FLIP THE GUMMI RING

TIME 20 minutes

SKILL LEVEL Get a grown-up

Can you turn a gummi candy upside-down—without touching it?

What you need:

Gummi peach ring candy with a marshmallow layer on the bottom, or other gummi marshmallow candy, such as gummi frogs

Baking sheet lined with parchment or aluminum foil

Oven

What to do:

1. Preheat the oven to 200°F.

2. Place the candy on the baking sheet, marshmallow side down.

3. Put the candy in the oven and check back every 5 minutes. What is happening to the bubbles?

4. After 20 minutes, take it out. Where is the marshmallow layer?

What's happening:

The marshmallow layer of the candy contains thousands of tiny bubbles. When you heat the candy, the bubbles rise through the melted candy and end up on top.

Bubbles rise through this melted gummi ring.

BUBBLES AND HEARTS

TIME Several hours

SKILL LEVEL Easy

Can you spear a conversation heart without shattering it?

What you need:

Conversation hearts

Clear dish of water

What to do:

1. Drop the hearts into the dish of water.

2. After several hours, check the hearts. What do they look like? What happens if you poke them with a spoon or a pin?

What's happening:

Conversation hearts are "tableted" candy, where a sugar mixture is compressed in a mold. Any air bubbles in the mixture get trapped inside.

When you dissolve conversation hearts, the sugars dissolve out. But some ingredients remain, such as gelatin and air. The heart looks perfectly solid, but if you touch it, you'll see that it's just a soft collection of bubbles.

Hours soaking in water have turned these hearts into a mass of bubbles.

WARTY LICORICE

TIME 5 minutes

SKILL LEVEL Get a grown-up

Can you make a smooth piece of licorice grow warts?

What you need:

Twizzlers licorice twists (the Pull-n-Peel variety works especially well)

Microwave-safe plate

Microwave

(Alternative: baking sheet lined with aluminum foil or parchment paper, and oven)

Microwaving this licorice gives it warts.

What to do:

1 Place the licorice on the plate.

2 Microwave on low or medium heat, checking it every 30 seconds so it doesn't start to burn. Does your licorice grow warts?

Alternative:

Place licorice on baking sheet and heat in 300°F oven. Check back every 5 minutes until you see warts growing.

What's happening:

Licorice, like most soft candy, contains a little water. The warts might be created by water making tiny pockets of steam when it's heated.

Why doesn't licorice melt in the oven or microwave? Because licorice contains flour, which doesn't melt. This also means that by some legal definitions, licorice isn't actually candy!

CRUSH POP ROCKS

TIME 5 minutes

SKILL LEVEL Easy

Pop Rocks are full of tiny air bubbles.
What happens when you crush them?

What you need:

Package of Pop Rocks, unopened

Rolling pin or mortar and pestle

What to do:

1. Hold the package of Pop Rocks and squash the candy inside with your fingers. Do you hear loud popping noises?

Alternatives:

- Lay the package on a flat surface and crush it with a rolling pin.
- Pour the Pop Rocks into a mortar, and crush them with a pestle. (This can cause some Pop Rocks to jump out of the bowl, so you might end up with a sticky counter.)

What's happening:

Pop Rocks contain tiny bubbles of carbon dioxide gas. When you crush the candy, you release the carbon dioxide, making a popping sound. It's like popping a thousand tiny balloons.

Crush Pop Rocks to release the bubbles.

Can you make Pop Rocks puff up into pearls?

What you need:

Pop Rocks

Baking sheet lined with aluminum foil or parchment paper

Oven

What to do:

1. Preheat the oven to 400°F.

2. Sprinkle Pop Rocks on the baking sheet.

3. Heat in oven for 2 to 5 minutes. Do the Pop Rocks look puffy?

What's happening:

Pop Rocks are made by pumping carbon dioxide into melted candy, then cooling the candy and trapping the bubbles. The gas in these bubbles is trapped at a very high pressure, which is why the candy crackles in your mouth when you eat it—all those high-pressure bubbles are exploding.

When you melt the Pop Rocks in the oven, the tiny bubbles expand and push on the soft, molten candy, making the Pop Rocks expand. The bubbles also get bigger, which is why the translucent Pop Rocks turn opaque and cloudy after heating.

These Pop Rocks
puff up in the oven.

UNBUBBLING POP ROCKS

Pop Rocks bubble in water. What about oil?

What you need:

Pop Rocks

Two clear glasses

Cooking oil, such as vegetable or olive oil

Water

What to do:

1. Pour water into one glass, and pour cooking oil into the second glass.

2. Add Pop Rocks to each glass. Do the Pop Rocks in water bubble and fizz? What about the Pop Rocks in oil?

Do Pop Rocks bubble in oil?

What's happening:

Pop Rocks are made of sugar, which dissolves in water. As the Pop Rocks dissolve, they release tiny trapped bubbles of carbon dioxide, which make the water bubble and make noise. But sugar doesn't dissolve in oil, so the Pop Rocks in oil don't dissolve or release bubbles. This is why Pop Rocks can be mixed with chocolate and still keep their bubbles, such as in Chocolate Pop Rocks or some specialty candy bars. They don't dissolve until you eat them!

If your bowl has any floating Pop Rocks, leave the bowl alone for several days. Do the Pop Rocks change shape or get sticky? Pop Rocks don't dissolve in oil, but they are hygroscopic, meaning they absorb water from the atmosphere. If the air is humid, the water starts to dissolve the Pop Rocks in the oil, causing them to flatten, stick together, or even drip to the bottom of the bowl.

Pop Rocks floating in oil absorb humidity and dissolve, dripping into the bowl.

Save this bowl for the Pop Rocks Bubble Trap experiment on page 82.

POP ROCKS BUBBLE TRAP

TIME 10 minutes

SKILL LEVEL Medium

Pop Rocks bubbles zoom upward. Can you slow them down?

What you need:

Pop Rocks

Small clear bowl

Cooking oil, such as vegetable or olive oil

Water

What to do:

1. Pour about 1 inch of oil into the bowl.

2. Pour the Pop Rocks into the bowl and let them sink to the bottom.

3. Slowly pour about ½ cup of water into the bowl. Watch for rising bubbles. Do they slow down when they reach the oil?

What's happening:

Pop Rocks don't dissolve in oil, but they do dissolve in water. When this happens, bubbles rise through the water and into the oil. Because oil is more viscous (sticky and thick) than water, the bubbles collect together and rise more slowly.

Oil traps the bubbles from
these dissolving Pop Rocks.

Look at the bowl from underneath, so you can see the surface of the oil.
Its surface makes a reflective layer, like a mirror. When you look at it from
underneath, sometimes the reflected bubbles look as if they're sinking
instead of rising.

even more fun

If you'd like to see your solution bubble faster, stir it!

POPCORN POP ROCKS

TIME 10 minutes

SKILL LEVEL Get a grown-up

With a little hot water, you can make these Pop Rocks really pop!

What you need:

Pop Rocks

Hot water (about 140°F)

A clear bottle with a narrow top, such as a water bottle with a flat bottom, a clear drinking glass, or a microwave-safe bowl (alternative)

Safety glasses

What to do:

1. Pour about a tablespoon of hot water into the bottle. Use just enough to cover the bottom of the bottle. (If you use too much water, the experiment won't work.)

2. If you're using a drinking glass instead of a bottle, put on the safety glasses.

3. Pour in some Pop Rocks and see if any jump!

Alternative:

Heat a little bit of water in a microwave-safe bowl, then pour out almost all of the water. (The bowl will keep the remaining water hot.) Put on safety glasses, and then pour in the Pop Rocks.

What's happening:

Pop Rocks are full of tiny trapped bubbles of carbon dioxide. The hot water dissolves the candy so fast that the air bubbles explode, making the Pop Rocks shoot up like popcorn.

Pop Rocks dropped in hot water jump out of the bowl.

SODA GEYSER SHOWDOWN

TIME 30 minutes

SKILL LEVEL Medium

Drop Mentos in Diet Coke, and you'll create a geyser that spouts as high as your house. Why do Mentos work so well? What other kinds of candy make a good soda geyser?

What you need:

Pieces of candy (any kind), such as Smarties, Altoids, M&M's, Mentos, or Bumpy Nerds jelly beans

Pixy Stix or sugar

Clear cups or bowls

Several bottles of diet soda (20-ounce bottles create less mess, but 2-liter bottles will make bigger geysers)

A tube for dropping the candy, such as the Steve Spangler Geyser Tube. (You can also make your own by cutting a toilet paper tube lengthwise, wrapping it around the Mentos tube, and taping it. Save a piece of cardboard to put underneath—this will hold up the candy until you're ready to release it.)

What to do:

1. To see what makes soda bubble the most, set several cups on a table and pour an equal amount of soda into each cup.

2. Pour the spoonful of sugar in one cup. Add the candy to the other cups, each kind in a different cup.

3. How many bubbles do you see? What makes the best bubbles?

4. To compare soda geysers, take the sode bottles outside or to a large open area.* Load your candy tube with the first kind of candy and place it on the soda bottle. When you're ready, release the candy and get out of the way as the geyser erupts. Repeat with every kind of candy. Which geyser goes the highest?

*If you try this experiment indoors, use small bottles of soda, place them on a tray to contain some of the mess, and prepare to mop up afterward.

What's happening:

Soda contains dissolved carbon dioxide gas. When it touches a surface, this gas turns into bubbles. Smooth candy doesn't produce as many bubbles as rough candy, because rough candy, with its edges and holes, has more surface area— more room for the bubbles to form. Mentos are covered with tiny pits, or holes, which make a good place for bubbles to form. Sugar also makes the soda fizz because each side of every tiny sugar crystal provides a place for bubbles to form.

Candy that makes soda fizz might not always make a good geyser. For instance, sugar isn't heavy enough to sink to the bottom of a soda bottle when bubbles are pushing out. Altoids also make good bubbles, but they get pushed out by erupting soda instead of sinking. Mentos, on the other hand, are so big and heavy that they sink through bubbling soda. They take up space in the soda bottle, forcing some of the soda out. Mentos also contain gum arabic, which reduces surface tension in the soda and makes it less able to stick together. This allows it to bubble higher.

Which kind of candy makes soda bubble most?

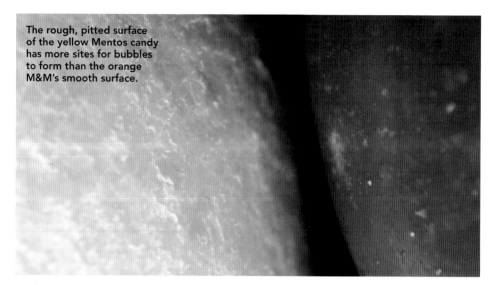

The rough, pitted surface of the yellow Mentos candy has more sites for bubbles to form than the orange M&M's smooth surface.

One other kind of candy can compete with Mentos in a geyser contest: Bumpy Nerds jelly beans. The bumps give each jelly bean more surface area, making more room for the all-important soda bubbles to form. This makes them a close competitor for making soda geysers.

Bumpy Nerds have more surface area, making them good for soda geysers.

science fair ideas

● Before you try the experiment, examine each kind of candy. Is the candy heavy or light? Will it sink or float? Is it very smooth, or slightly rough? Use your observations to predict what kind of candy will make the biggest geyser.

An erupting Mentos
soda geyser.

DIVING CANDY

TIME 5 minutes

SKILL LEVEL Easy

Can you make a piece of candy dive and then surface again?

What you need:

Warheads (recommended), or other candy that is sealed in plastic, such as a Gobstopper or striped mint. Do not unwrap! The candy wrapper must be sealed on both edges, not just twisted tight.

A plastic bottle with a tight-fitting lid, filled to the brim with water. (Soda bottles work better than juice or syrup bottles.)

Water

Bowl (optional)

Pin (optional)

Needle-nose pliers (optional)

What to do:

1. Drop the wrapped candy into the bottle of water. (If you're using a bottle with a narrow neck, you may have to gently push the candy through the opening.) Does the candy float?

2. If the candy floats, tightly fasten the lid of the bottle.

3. Squeeze the bottle. Does the candy sink? *(Hint: Small hands might have a hard time squeezing the bottle hard enough to make the candy dive. To try another method, lay the bottle down sideways on the floor and stand on it.)*

4. If the candy does not sink, try one of these fixes:
   a. Using needle-nose pliers, pull the candy out of the bottle. Use a pin to poke a tiny hole in the wrapper, near an edge or the bottom. Put the candy back in the bottle, with the hole on the bottom side. The wrapper should slowly start to fill with water, trapping an air bubble at the top of the wrapper.
   b. Try a different piece of candy.
   c. Try a different bottle, such as a small soda bottle that is easy to squeeze.

What's happening:

Most candy is denser than water, so it sinks. But if air is trapped inside the wrapper, the wrapped candy floats.

To float, a piece of candy has to push aside more than its weight in water. Candy is denser (heavier) than water, and so it sinks. But if a piece of candy is in a wrapper filled with air, it is lighter than the equivalent volume of water, and it floats.

When you squeeze the bottle, the water squeezes the candy. The air bubble trapped inside the wrapper gets smaller. The candy pushes aside less water, and the water no longer supports it. The candy sinks. When you stop pushing the bottle, the air bubble expands (gets bigger). The wrapper pushes aside more water, and the candy floats.

Some fish have a swim bladder that functions the same way. When they contract the air-filled bladder, the fish descend. When they let the air sac expand, they rise. Other fish adjust their buoyancy by letting air in and out of the swim bladder, making it bigger or smaller. This helps the fish swim up and down.

Note: Since every piece of candy is wrapped differently, some of them will not float, and some of them will not sink. You may have to try several pieces of candy to get the right air bubble. But when it works, it's really fun.

You can also try this with a packet of ketchup, mustard, or soy sauce.

Squeezing the bottle makes the candy dive.

VOCABULARY

Cartesian diver: a floating object inside a bottle that sinks when pressure is applied, named after French philosopher René Descartes.

Light passes through a window, making it transparent. Light scatters a little as it passes through a Jolly Rancher, making it translucent. Light bounces off of a chocolate bar, making it opaque.

Light also gets bent by substances such as glass and water. This is what makes a spoon or a straw look so funny when you see it through the side of a water glass. Light can even bend in ways that make objects seem to disappear.

Read this chapter to explore playing with light.

7

LIGHT

CAN SUGAR WATER BEND LIGHT?

TIME 5 minutes

SKILL LEVEL Easy

How can you bend a straw without touching it?

What you need:

Clear glass of water

Sugar

Straw, pen, licorice, or something else tall and straight

What to do:

1 Add a few spoonfuls of sugar to the glass of water. Wait a few minutes. Do not stir!

2 Put the straw in the glass. What does the bottom end of the straw look like?

What's happening:

When you add sugar to water, you change the way that the water bends light (the index of refraction). The more sugar you add, the bigger the change. If the sugar water remains at the bottom of the glass, the straw appears to bend where it enters the denser sugar solution.

Remember that the sugar water isn't the only thing making the straw look bent. Your round glass also bends light. Try turning the glass and looking at it from different angles to see if you can tell whether it's the sugar water or the glass itself that changes the way the straw looks.

At home, bending light with sugar water is just a fun trick. But in many businesses, measuring the index of refraction is a useful tool. Sellers of soda, wine, or honey often measure refractive index to calculate how much sugar a substance contains, which they use to predict how sweet it will be.

A straw "bending" in sugar water.

more fun

Try this with a glass of fresh water, or a glass of water with candy in it. How do they compare? Which bends light the most?

VOCABULARY

Index of refraction: a measurement of how fast light passes through a substance. This determines how much the substance will bend light.

SUGAR WATER SWIRLS

TIME 10 minutes

SKILL LEVEL Easy

Because sugar water bends light, you can use it to make beautiful liquid swirls.

What you need:

Sugar or xylitol

Clear glass of water

Hard, clear candies like Warheads or Jolly Ranchers (alternative)

What to do:

1. Add a spoonful of sugar or xylitol to the glass of water, and stir until dissolved.

2. Pour some more water into the same glass. Do you see swirls?

Alternative:

Pour water into a clear glass, then add either a spoonful of sugar or a few hard, clear candies (like Warheads or Jolly Ranchers). Do not stir. When the substance has dissolved as much as it can, gently move the glass back and forth. Do you see swirls in the middle of the glass where the dense sugar water mixes with the less-dense water?

What's happening:

Although water and sugar water are both transparent, they bend light in different ways. (They each have a different index of refraction.) When you pour them together, the light bends where the two liquids meet, allowing you to see the swirls of moving water as they mix.

Adding water to a sugar
solution makes swirls.

INVISIBLE LICORICE

TIME
5 minutes

SKILL LEVEL
Easy

Can you make candy disappear without eating it?

What you need:

Licorice, or other long, straight candy (alternative: a pencil or straw)

Tall, skinny drinking glass

Cooking oil, such as vegetable or olive oil

What to do:

1. Pour some oil into the glass.

2. Put the candy stick into the glass. At the surface of the oil, does the candy look as if it has been cut in half?

3. Lean the candy stick against the side of the glass. (If the licorice doesn't lay flat against the side, make a bend near the bottom of the stick to help hold it in place.)

4. Look at the side of the glass, and slowly turn it. Does the licorice get wider and narrower? Can you make it disappear?

What's happening:

You've probably noticed how light bends in a glass of water. This is what makes things inside a glass of water look so distorted and strange.

Oil bends light even more than water does. In fact, it can bend the light so much that, if you hold the glass the right way, a piece of candy nestled against the side of the glass is completely hidden from your eyes.

Oil refracting
the light makes
this licorice
"disappear."

more fun

Pour some water into the same glass and look again. Now the candy
looks sliced in two both where the oil meets the air and where the oil
meets the water. Turn the glass around. Does the candy look different in
the water or the oil?

COTTON CANDY STAINED GLASS

With a little oil, you can turn opaque cotton candy translucent.

What you need:

Cotton candy

Bowl

Cooking oil, such as vegetable or olive oil

What to do:

1. Look at your cotton candy. Does it look translucent or opaque? (Can you see light through it, or not?)

2. Pour some oil in the bowl.

3. Dip the cotton candy in the oil, or set the candy in the bowl to let it absorb oil. (If you get oil on your hands, wash them with soap right away. Oil can stain clothes.)

4. After a few minutes look at the candy again. Does it look translucent or opaque?

What's happening:

Individual strands of cotton candy are transparent, like glass. But every time light goes through a strand, it bends where the candy touches the air. This causes the light to bounce around in many different directions, instead of passing straight through the candy. This is why cotton candy looks opaque.

Oil has a closer index of refraction to sugar than air does. When candy touches oil, the light doesn't bend as much as when it touches air. The light passes through the candy more easily, making it look translucent.

This is also the reason that paper soaked in oil turns more translucent. Many pioneers used oiled paper or cloth to make translucent windows, because glass was too expensive.

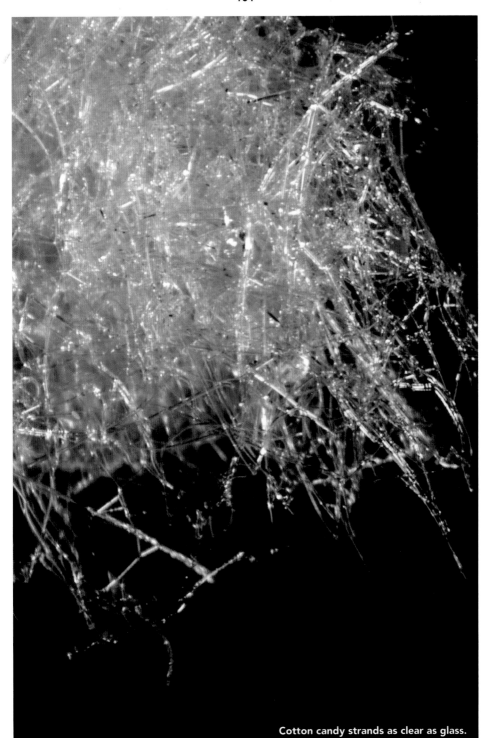

Cotton candy strands as clear as glass.

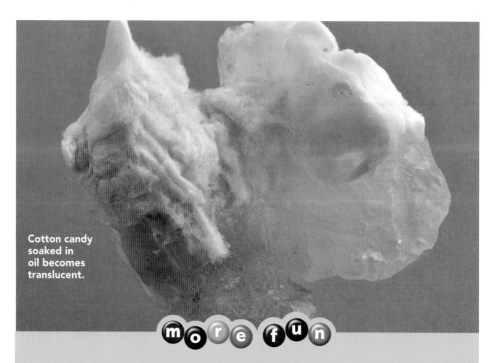

Cotton candy
soaked in
oil becomes
translucent.

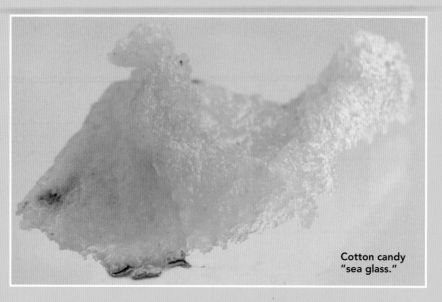

m o r e f u n

Sometimes you can mold oily cotton candy into different shapes like sea glass, the kind of translucent, foggy glass you find on beaches. What sea glass shapes can you make with your cotton candy?

Cotton candy
"sea glass."

GHOSTLY GUMMIES

TIME 2 days

SKILL LEVEL Easy

How do you make a gummi bear start to disappear?

What you need:

Gummi candy

Clear dish of water

What to do:

1. Put the gummi candy in the dish of water.

2. Check your gummi candy after several hours. Does it look as if the edges are starting to fade?

3. Wait up to 2 days. Does the candy turn see-through?

What's happening:

As the candy expands, the dyes in the candy are less concentrated. Some of the dye even dissolves into the water, making the gummi candy more translucent, so that light passes through more easily. Get the candy big enough, and it can become transparent enough for you to read print through it!

You might also notice more variations of color in your gummi candy. As you expand it, you can see places where the dye is more or less concentrated, making colored swirls and streaks inside the candy.

As dye dissolves out of this gummi bear, it starts to disappear.

VANISHING GUMMIES

TIME 2 days

SKILL LEVEL Medium

How do you make a gummi bear disappear entirely?

What you need:

Gummi candy that is completely or partly light-colored, such as pineapple gummi bears, red-and-clear gummi worms, or cola bottle gummi candy

Clear dish of water

What to do:

1. Put the gummi candy in the dish of water.

2. Wait up to 2 days. Does the clear part of the candy start to disappear?

3. Sometimes air bubbles form on the surface of the candy, making the candy's outline more visible. To get rid of the bubbles, try gently lifting the candy out of the water to let the bubbles pop. Then put the candy back in the water and look again.

4. Some gummi candy is clear but has rough edges that show up in water. In this case, gently break your gummi in half. Use a small spoon to scoop out tiny pieces from the inside of the candy, and put them back in water. Do they disappear?

What's happening:

Water bends light. So do other translucent substances, such as oil, soda, and gummi worms. When one of these substances touches another, it creates a place where light bends. That's why if you put a small glass bowl in a larger bowl of water, you can still see the glass.

When the gelatin has absorbed as much water as it can, it bends light nearly the same way water does. That allows it to blend right into the water.

This gummi bear sits on invisible waterlogged legs.

more fun

If you don't have light-colored gummi candy, mix up some plain gelatin according to the package instructions, let it solidify, and scoop out pieces to experiment with. It also makes ghostly shapes in the water.

THE GUMMI GECKO

TIME 2 days

SKILL LEVEL Easy

**Most gummi candy is translucent, but this gecko is opaque.
Can you guess why?
(Hint: this also makes the gummi gecko a good swimmer!)**

What you need:

Sour Gecko gummi candy

Clear baking dish filled with about 2 inches of water

What to do:

1 Put the gummi gecko into the dish of water.

2 Wait 2 days. What do you see?

What's happening:

As the gummi gecko absorbs water, it expands. As it expands, you can start to see what's trapped inside: tiny air bubbles. These air bubbles scatter light instead of letting it pass through the gummi, helping to make the gummi gecko opaque. They also help it float!

Does this mean that all opaque gummies contain air bubbles? No. Gummies can also contain the white food coloring titanium dioxide to make them look solid instead of translucent.

What makes this gummi gecko opaque?

Shake the dish gently from side to side. Can you make your gecko swim?

TRANSLUCENT TAFFY

TIME 30 minutes

SKILL LEVEL Get a grown-up

Can you turn taffy translucent?

What you need:

Saltwater taffy, Laffy Taffy, or other opaque fruity chew

Foil-lined baking sheet

Oven

What to do:

1. Preheat the oven to about 300°F.

2. Place the unwrapped candy on the baking sheet.

3. Heat the candy in the oven for up to 30 minutes, checking every few minutes. What does the candy look like?

What's happening:

Have you ever watched a taffy-pulling machine? Metal arms stretch and fold the soft candy, stretching and folding it over and over. As this happens, tiny air bubbles get trapped in the taffy, making it soft and chewy. (Without the air bubbles to separate the sugar molecules, the taffy would be as hard as a lollipop.)

The air bubbles also break up light rays when they pass through. Instead of passing right through the candy, the light gets absorbed or refracted by the air bubbles, making the candy look cloudy. When you melt it into a thin puddle, and some of the air bubbles escape, the taffy becomes translucent again.

Can you make this taffy translucent?

TURN PIXY STIX TRANSLUCENT

TIME
30 minutes

SKILL LEVEL
Get a grown-up

Can you see through Pixy Stix powder?

What you need:
Pixy Stix or Baby Bottle sour powder

Baking sheet lined with foil or parchment paper

Oven

Sugar (alternative)

What to do:
1. Heat the oven to 300°F.

2. Pour a pile of Pixy Stix onto the baking sheet.

3. Heat in the oven for up to 20 minutes.

4. Check the Pixy Stix every few minutes. Has the powder started to melt? Is it turning translucent?

Alternative:
Try this by heating sugar at 400°F.

What's happening:
The tiny crystals of dextrose and citric acid that make up Pixy Stix scatter light every time they touch the air. Where the surface of the crystal meets the air, the light bends. A pile of tiny crystals scatters the light and looks opaque.

When you melt the crystals, the candy melts together. It also gets smaller, because the air trapped in the pile of dust is released when the candy melts together. With fewer places for the candy to meet the air and scatter light, the pile of Pixy Stix turns translucent.

A little heat turns this Pixy Stix dust translucent.

MELT CHOCOLATE WITH A MAGNIFYING GLASS

TIME 10 minutes

SKILL LEVEL Get a grown-up

Can you bend enough light to melt chocolate?

What you need:

Chocolate bar

Magnifying glass (even a small one will do)

Sunshine

What to do:

1. Hold the magnifying glass over the unwrapped chocolate bar. Move it up and down until you see a small, bright circle of light. **(CAUTION— this can get hot!)**

2. Wait several seconds. Does the chocolate start to melt? (If you can't see a change, poke it to see if has softened.)

   When the bar has cooled again, look at the surface. Is it still shiny, or has it gotten dull?

What's happening:

A magnifying glass is curved on both sides. When light reaches the curved surface of the glass, it bends. When it leaves the glass, it bends again. The glass focuses the sun's light and heat in one place, melting your chocolate.

Why isn't the chocolate bar shiny after it melts? Because chocolate molecules can arrange themselves in many kinds of crystals. One formation makes shiny, crisp chocolate. Other formations of crystals cause the surface to go dull. Eventually the ingredients will start to separate, causing "chocolate bloom."

Can you use this light to carve up a chocolate bar? Sadly, no. The light only heats the chocolate—it doesn't carve or move it (even though so many movies show lasers blasting people off their feet).

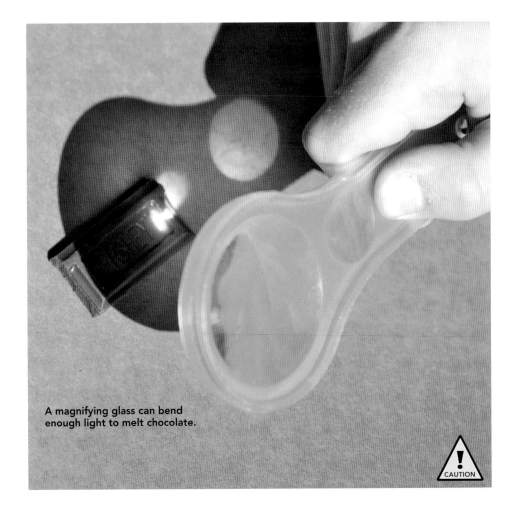

A magnifying glass can bend enough light to melt chocolate.

CAUTION

When molecules lock together in a regular pattern, they create crystals. Sometimes these crystals are translucent like jewels. Sometimes you can't see the crystals, such as in chocolate. Sometimes the crystals form slowly, sometimes they form quickly, and sometimes they form instantly.

Several of the experiments in this chapter use xylitol. Xylitol is a low-calorie sweetener available at many grocery stores. After you're done with the experiments, you can use the xylitol to sweeten other things. Since it has fewer calories than sugar and doesn't cause cavities, it may make a good substitute for sugar.

To dissolve the candy for these experiments, you'll need to heat it in water. Ask a grown-up to help you, since these mixtures will be very hot.

If you want to try making more crystals, or bigger crystals, double the amounts used in each experiment. The experiments will still work if you use the same proportions. (For instance, an experiment with 1 tablespoon of water and 1 tablespoon of xylitol will also work with 2 tablespoons of water and 2 tablespoons of xylitol.)

Get ready to make crystals and take them apart!

8

CRYSTALS

UN-BROWN SUGAR

TIME About 2 weeks

SKILL LEVEL Get a grown-up

Can you turn brown sugar into white sugar?

What you need:

Brown sugar

Small microwavable bowl with 1 tablespoon of water

Microwave

What to do:

1. Mix 2 tablespoons of brown sugar with the water in the bowl.

2. Microwave 15 to 30 seconds or until sugar dissolves. **(CAUTION—hot!)**

3. Wait several days and watch for crystals. What color are the crystals? Where did the brown color go?

What's happening:

Although brown sugar looks and tastes a lot different than white sugar (sucrose), it's almost the same. In fact, brown sugar is just white sugar with a little bit of molasses that adds flavor, color, and moisture. (Sugar produced by sugar cane already contains molasses. When the sugar is processed, sometimes the molasses is left with the sugar to make brown sugar. Other brown sugars are made by adding molasses to white sugar after it is processed.)

When you dissolve the sugar, the sucrose molecules separate and mix with the water. As the water evaporates, these molecules lock together to form crystals. But there's no room in this crystalline structure for other kinds of molecules. The white sugar crystallizes together, leaving the molasses at the bottom of the bowl.

This doesn't only happen with sugar. Most molecules will only form crystals with their own kind. This makes crystallization a good way for chemists to purify compounds (separate out one compound from other kinds).

Brown molasses drips from
crystallizing sugar.

CHOCOLATE SAWDUST

TIME
Several days
to two years

SKILL LEVEL
Medium

Chocolate is held together by its crystal structure. When the crystals in chocolate make the right formation, the ingredients stay stable. But if you break up the crystals, watch out!

What you need:

Chocolate, such as a small chocolate bar

Heat source, such as a microwave, low oven, or hair dryer

An out-of-the-way hiding spot, such as the back of a cupboard or the top of your fridge

What to do:

1. Start the process of chocolate bloom by heating the chocolate until it starts to melt. You can use a microwave, a low oven, a hair dryer, or even a sunny windowsill. (Chocolate melts fast. If it doesn't look melted, poke it with a fork to check.)

2. After the chocolate cools, check for light streaks. (It can take anywhere from a few hours to a few days for the streaks to form.) These streaks are made of cocoa butter.

3. Wait several days or weeks.

4. Examine your chocolate and try to break it. Is it getting brittle and crumbly?

Optional: Set aside your chocolate for 2 years. By the end, you might have a pile of chocolate sawdust!

What's happening:

Chocolate is made of cocoa butter, cocoa solids, sugar, and other ingredients. When you buy chocolate from the store, it has been tempered. That means it has been melted and cooled at the right temperature for the right crystals to form, holding all the ingredients in place. If you heat the chocolate, the crystals break apart and re-form in other, less stable formations. The white cocoa butter starts to separate out (causing chocolate bloom), and the chocolate becomes more brittle. As time passes, the crystals separate more and more. Wait long enough, and the chocolate can crumble into sawdust.

Does two years seem like too long to wait? If you melt chocolate and stir in a little bit of water, the water will interfere with the bonds between the chocolate molecules. The cooled chocolate will be more crumbly and brittle than good chocolate. (See the Seize Chocolate experiment on page 46.)

Chocolate bars crumbling into sawdust.

ICE CRYSTALS

**One brand of xylitol candy is named Ice Chips.
Are they really made of ice?**

What you need:

Ice Chips brand candy, smashed into small pieces, or granulated xylitol

Small clear bowl with 1 tablespoon of water

Thermometer (optional)

What to do:

1. Add 1 tablespoon of xylitol to the bowl of water.

2. Touch the solution, or use a thermometer to take the temperature. Does it feel cold?

What's happening:

Ice Chips aren't really made from ice. But xylitol does cool water down when it dissolves. Xylitol molecules fit together so well in crystal form that it takes a lot of energy to separate and dissolve them. This means that when you dissolve xylitol, the xylitol absorbs energy from the water, making the water colder. When xylitol crystallizes, it releases energy and heats the water (see the Instant Crystallization experiment on page 122).

Xylitol "frost."

more fun

Here's another way to make xylitol resemble ice. Mix 1 tablespoon of water with 3 tablespoons of xylitol in a small bowl, heating and stirring until the xylitol dissolves completely. Pour the solution into a second bowl and put both bowls aside for several hours. Does the thin film of xylitol crystallize into feathery patterns like frost?

CANDY DIAMONDS

Can you make candy that looks like jewels?

What you need:

Ice Chips brand candy or granulated xylitol

Small clear microwave-safe bowl with 1 tablespoon of water

Microwave

What to do:

1. Mix 2 tablespoons of xylitol into the bowl of water.

2. Microwave the mixture for 15 to 30 seconds and stir. Repeat until the xylitol has dissolved.

3. Wait for a few days. Do you see crystals forming?

What's happening:

Crystals form when molecules that are dissolved in solution start turning solid again. If there is already a solid crystal in the water, the dissolved xylitol molecules can easily fit into place, making the crystal grow bigger.

To help your crystals grow bigger, try removing any extra crystals. You can also mix up a new batch of xylitol and water, and move your best crystals into the new solution once it has cooled down. If there are fewer crystals in the solution, those crystals will grow bigger.

Quick crystals:

The more xylitol you add to the water, the faster it forms crystals. Experiment by mixing xylitol and water in different amounts. Can you make crystals that develop in less than a day? In less than an hour?

A xylitol crystal.

INSTANT CRYSTALLIZATION

TIME
1 hour

SKILL LEVEL
Get a grown-up

What happens if you dissolve so much xylitol the water can't hold it all? Things really start to heat up!

What you need:

Granulated xylitol (recommended) or Ice Chips candy

Water

Small clear, microwave-safe bowl

Microwave

Kitchen scale (optional)

Thermometer (optional)

What to do:

1. Mix 4 grams of water (1 teaspoon) and 22 grams of xylitol (about 2 tablespoons, but it will be more accurate if you measure with a kitchen scale).

2. Microwave 15 to 30 seconds until the water is hot, then stir. Repeat until all the xylitol has dissolved.

3. Wait several minutes for the solution to cool.

4. Stir the solution and wait about a minute. Does anything start to happen? If not, sprinkle in a few grains of xylitol and stir again. Do you see spirals where you stirred? Does the solution start to turn white?

   As the solution crystallizes, feel the side of the bowl, or use a thermometer to measure the temperature. **(Careful—this solution can get very hot.)**

   If the experiment doesn't work, heat it up again and try this:

   - Pour the warm solution into a clean bowl. (This will prevent crystals from forming around any xylitol grains stuck to the side of the bowl.)
   - If you see crystals developing as the solution cools, heat and stir to dissolve the crystals.

What's happening:

When you dissolve lots of xylitol in hot water, the solution becomes saturated. Cool it down, and it contains more dissolved xylitol than it should be able to hold. But without a seed crystal for the dissolved molecules to lock onto, they stay dissolved. The solution is supersaturated.

When you add a seed crystal, or stir the solution, the crystallization process starts. For a supersaturated xylitol solution, this process can happen quickly. There are so many dissolved molecules ready to form crystals that the whole solution can crystallize within minutes.

Why does the solution heat up? Xylitol molecules lock together so well that it takes a lot of energy to separate and dissolve them. This is why water cools down when xylitol dissolves (see the Ice Crystals experiment on page 118). The energy is then contained in the solution. When the xylitol molecules join back together, energy is released, making the water warm.

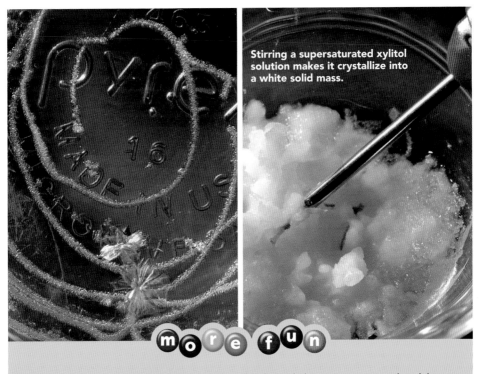

Stirring a supersaturated xylitol solution makes it crystallize into a white solid mass.

more fun

Reheat the solution to dissolve the xylitol, and do it again. You should be able to reuse the same xylitol several times without adding any more water.

Jousting Peeps, marshmallow launchers, and dry ice that makes marshmallows shatter like glass. Go a little crazy with candy experiments!

9

JUST FOR FUN

JOUSTING PEEPS

TIME 10 minutes

SKILL LEVEL Get a grown-up

In medieval jousts, knights used heavy armor, lances, and warhorses. Today there's an easier way to joust: with Peeps.

What you need:

Peeps candy, or regular marshmallows

Microwave-safe plate

Toothpicks

Microwave

What to do:

1. Place two Peeps marshmallows on a plate, facing each other.

2. Stick a toothpick in each, pointing at the other Peep.

3. Microwave and watch the Peeps expand. The Peep that pricks the other one is the winner.

What's happening:

Peeps are made of marshmallows, which contain sugar, gelatin, air, and water. When the water turns to steam, the air pockets expand, making the Peeps grow.

Sometimes a Peeps marshmallow will collapse when it gets pricked. This might be because the steam can escape more easily.

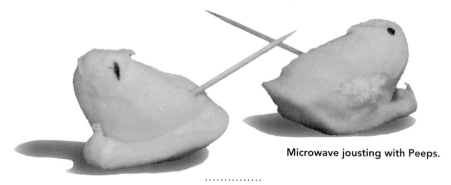

Microwave jousting with Peeps.

SUGAR-FREE TIC TACS?

Tic Tacs are made from sugar. So how can the label claim
that they have no sugar per serving?

What you need:

Package of Tic Tacs

Is there sugar in these
Tic Tacs or not?

What to do:

1 Read the ingredients list. What's
the first ingredient?

2 Read the nutrition label. How much
sugar is listed?

What's happening:

When writing nutrition labels, manu-
facturers are allowed to round down.
This allows the label to claim that a Tic
Tac weighing 0.49 grams has 0 grams
of sugar.

more fun

Do you need proof that Tic Tacs contain sugar? Try chewing wintergreen
Tic Tacs in front of a mirror in a dark room. Like wintergreen Life Savers,
Tic Tacs occasionally flash when they're chewed or broken. This happens
because breaking the sugar crystals causes the electrons to move,
creating flashes.

MARSHMALLOW BOTTLE LAUNCHER

TIME 10 minutes

SKILL LEVEL Easy

How far can you shoot a marshmallow?

What you need:

Large marshmallow

Clean, empty plastic drink bottle, such as a 2-liter soda bottle

What to do:

1 Push the marshmallow into the opening of the bottle so that it's sticking out. You might need to use your fingers to gently shove the edges of the marshmallow all the way into the opening.

2 Squeeze or stomp on the bottle. Does the marshmallow pop out?

What's happening:

When you squeeze the soda bottle, you compress the air trapped inside. The air pushes against the marshmallow, shooting it out.

Launching a marshmallow.

What kind of bottle shoots marshmallows the best? Why?

DO MINT AND ORANGE MIX?

TIME 10 minutes

SKILL LEVEL Easy

Can mint affect the taste of other foods?

What you need:

Mint-flavored candy, gum, or toothpaste

Slice of an orange, or glass of orange juice

What to do:

1. Taste the mint flavor by eating a mint, chewing your gum, or brushing your teeth.

2. Taste a slice of orange or a glass of orange juice. How does it taste?

What's happening:

Mint flavor can interfere with our enjoyment of other flavors, especially acidic flavors like those in fruit. It may be that the "cooling" effect of the mint gum sensitizes the nerves that also taste the citric acid, so that the orange tastes more acidic (or sour). Mint toothpaste also has other ingredients that might interfere with the way we taste sweetness.

The way mint affects taste might explain why mint gum doesn't seem to help people eat more healthy food. Researchers in a recent study wondered if people chewing gum would eat less, or cut down on calories. The gum-chewers in the study ate fewer snacks, but ate bigger meals, and actually ate less healthy food such as fruit. This might be because mint gum doesn't interfere with the taste of fat and salt, but it can make healthy snacks like fruit taste bad.

Can you eat mint and orange together?

science fair ideas

- Is there a kind of toothpaste that doesn't affect our taste for healthy food?
- Which kind of mint most changes the flavor of orange—mint candy, gum, or toothpaste?
- Is there a kind of non-mint gum that helps people snack less or eat healthy food?
- What other things affect taste? Ask your friends to eat different kinds of foods, such as salty potato chips, sour lemon juice, or spicy hot sauce, then sample different flavors to see if the taste has changed. Do any of your test foods enhance or hide other flavors?

DO CHOCOLATE PEANUTS MAKE CHOCOLATE PEANUT BUTTER?

Peanut butter is made by grinding peanuts to release the peanut oil. Is chocolate peanut butter made the same way?

What you need:

Chocolate peanut candy, such as a chocolate peanut bar, peanut M&M's, or chocolate-covered peanuts

Blender, food processor, or mortar and pestle

What to do:

1. Put the candy in the blender, food processor, or mortar.

2. Grind the candy into tiny pieces. Does it stick together like peanut butter, or does it turn sandy?

What's happening:

Peanuts turn to peanut butter when you grind them into small particles, releasing the peanut oil. But ground chocolate is still solid chocolate, because it's at room temperature. It can't stick together to make a spread.

Next time you buy a bottle of chocolate nut spread, check the label. It probably contains cocoa powder instead of solid chocolate, which makes a chocolatey paste when mixed with added oils. The picture on the label might show nuts and chocolate, but you're probably getting a few extra ingredients. And don't forget about the other main ingredient in chocolate nut spread—sugar.

Ingredients for chocolate peanut butter?

more fun

If you do grind up chocolate peanut candy, is there a way to turn it into a paste? What if you add vegetable oil? What if you heat it?

COTTON CANDY SUGAR SHOWDOWN

TIME minutes

SKILL LEVEL Easy

**Cotton candy is made almost entirely from sugar.
Is it the most sugary snack you can have?**

What you need:

A serving of cotton candy, such as the standard football-sized puff on a paper stick

Kitchen scale

Sugary snacks or drinks

Plastic bag (optional)

What to do:

1. Weigh the cotton candy on the kitchen scale. How much does it weigh? (You can put it in the plastic bag to weigh it, but remember to subtract the weight of the bag from the total amount.)

2. Check the sugar content in other snacks and drinks. How does it compare?

What's happening:

Since cotton candy is mostly air, each bite has less sugar than you might think. In fact, a large soda might have more sugar than your stick of cotton candy!

WHAT KIND OF CANDY LASTS LONGEST?

TIME 10 minutes to several weeks

SKILL LEVEL Easy

If you have a big pile of candy, you might have to decide what to use first and what to save. How do you decide?

What you need:

Old candy, including soft candy like taffy; clear, hard candy such as Jolly Ranchers; and sugar candy such as Altoids, Tic Tacs, or Smarties

What to do:

1. Find some old candy. (If you don't have any old candy, try hiding several kinds of candy in a humid environment, such as your bathroom, for several weeks.)

2. Unwrap and compare your candies. Do they look new, or do they look different? Have they changed color? Turned sticky? Turned hard? Is one kind of candy more affected than another?

What's happening:

How long candy lasts depends on what it's made of and whether it contains water.

Candy with a crystalline structure ages better than candy with a glassy structure. This means that candies made of crystalline sugar, like Altoids, or made of dextrose, like conversation hearts, are very stable. They don't absorb water from the atmosphere or degrade quickly.

In glassy candies, such as Jolly Ranchers or other clear candies made with corn syrup, the sugar molecules are not arranged into stable crystals. Instead, they are jumbled together with no organization and are more likely to bond to water from the atmosphere. This means that if a glass candy isn't fully wrapped, or if there's a hole in the package, the candy will eventually turn sticky. On the other hand, soft candies containing moisture might dry out and become hard.

Which candy is older?

more fun

When candy absorbs water from the air, it can get heavier. Can you use a kitchen scale to weigh various pieces of old and new candy and predict if any have absorbed water? (You might need a scale sensitive enough to weigh changes of 0.1 grams.) Once you open them, you'll know which is which, because the ones that have absorbed water should be sticky.

SHATTER FROZEN MARSHMALLOWS

TIME
30 minutes

SKILL LEVEL
Get a grown-up

Marshmallows are soft and squishy. Can you shatter them?

What you need:

Dry ice (available at many supermarkets)

Thick gloves or hot pads for handling the dry ice

Marshmallows

Tongs

Spoon

Hammer, or mortar and pestle

Small cooler (optional)

What to do:

1. Ask a grown-up to put the dry ice in the cooler. (The cooler will preserve the dry ice and help freeze the marshmallow.)

2. Lay a marshmallow on the dry ice.

3. Wait several minutes and let it freeze.

4. Have the grown-up use tongs or a spoon to pick up the marshmallow. Poke it with another spoon. What does it feel like?

5. Put the marshmallow on a baking sheet and smash it with something hard, such as a hammer. You can also try breaking it with a mortar and pestle. What happens?

What's happening:

The warmer molecules get, the more they move around. This is why, when you heat something like water, it will first become a liquid and then a gas.

When molecules get colder, they move around less. This is especially noticeable in an elastic substance like marshmallows, made from gelatin, sugar, and water. When you freeze the marshmallow, the molecules get locked into place. The marshmallow becomes a brittle solid. Smash it, and it breaks into fragments, just like any other piece of ice.

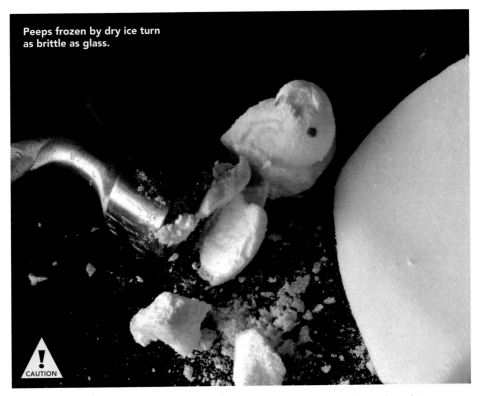

Peeps frozen by dry ice turn as brittle as glass.

CAUTION: If you touch or pick up dry ice, it can cause serious frostbite. Always ask grown-ups to handle dry ice for you, and remind them to use gloves or tongs.

Try this with any soft candy.

A frozen Cadbury Egg
shatters into pieces.

INDEX

acids and bases, 1–13
  explanation, xiv
air bubbles, 72–91
Altoids, 136–37
  bubble experiment, 86–89

Baby Bottle sour powder, light
  experiment, 108–9
brittle frozen candy, 140–41
brown sugar, 114–15
bubble experiments, 72–91
Bumpy Nerds jelly beans, bubble
  experiment, 86–89

Cadbury Easter egg, 56–57
candy ice, 30–31
Cartesian diver, 91
chocolate
  crystal experiment, 116–17
  light experiment, 110–11
  melting experiment, 34–35
  peanuts, 132–33
  seizing, 46–47
  water absorption experiment, 48–49
  water discoloring, 48–49
cocoa butter, 43
color experiments
  gummi candies, 2–3
  water discoloring chocolate, 48–49

conversation hearts
  acids and bases experiment, 8–9
  bubble experiment, 75
  dissolving experiment, 30–31
  melting experiment, 34–35, 75
cotton candy
  density experiment, 60–61
  dissolving experiments, 26–27, 28–29
  light experiment, 100–2
  sugar content, 134–35
  water absorption experiment, 42–43
"Crest Eggsperiment," 13
crystal experiments, 112–23

density experiments, 58–71, 88
diet soda, 86–89
dissolving experiments, 10–31
dry ice, 139, 140–41

Easter Grass candy, 44–45
eggshell dissolving, 10–13
experiment tips, x–xi

floating and sinking experiments. *See*
  density experiments
fluoride, 13
freezing points, 31

INDEX

geyser, soda, xi, 86–89
Gobstopper, 90
granulated xylitol. *See* xylitol
gummi candies
    acids and bases experiments, 2–3
    bubble experiment, 74
    color experiments, 2–3
    density experiment, 64–65
    dissolving experiments, 24–25
    dyeing, 50–51
    light experiments, 103, 104–5, 106
    melting experiments, 38, 39
    saltwater soak experiment, 52–53

Haribo frog, 64–65
hygroscopic, 81

ice, 30–31. *See also* dry ice
Ice Chips candy, crystal experiments,
    118–19, 120–21, 122–23
index of refraction, 94, 95

jawbreakers, dissolving experiment, 30–31
Jolly Ranchers, 136–37
    acids and bases experiment, 8–9
    dissolving experiment, 18–19, 30–31

Laffy Taffy, 107
Lemonheads
    dissolving experiment, 20–21
    pH tests, 4–5
licorice
    bubble experiment, 76
    light experiment, 98–99
light experiments, 92–111
lollipops, 22
longest lasting candy, 136–37

magnifying glass, 110–11
marshmallows. *See also* Peeps
  marshmallow candies
    bottle launcher, 128–29
    melting, 36–37
    shattering dried, 54–55
    shattering frozen, 138–39
melting experiments, 32–39, 75
Mentos, bubble experiment, 86–89
Milky Way bar, sinking, 62–63
mint and orange mix, 130–31
M&Ms
    bubble experiment, 86–89
    peanut, 132

Nerds
    acids and bases experiment, 8–9
    dissolving experiment, 18–19, 20–21
non-mint gum for less snacking, 131

INDEX

orange and mint mix, 130–31
osmosis, 52

peanut butter, 132–33
peanuts, 132–33
Peeps marshmallow candies, 126
    dissolving experiment, 23
    melting experiment, 36–37
    shattering, 54–55
pH tests, 4–5
Pixy Stix
    dissolving experiments, 16–17, 18–19
    light experiment, 108–9
    soda geyser experiment, 86–89
Pop Rocks
    acids and bases experiment, 6
    bubble experiments, 77, 78–79, 80–81,
        82–83, 84–85
    crushing, 77
    density experiment, 68–69, 70–71

refraction, 94–97, 100

salt, 31
saltwater, 52–53
    taffy, 107

saturated, 19
sawdust, chocolate, 116–17
science fair projects, xii–xiii
    "Crest Eggsperiment," 13
    eggshell dissolving, 13
    floating, 88
    freezing points, 31
    Gummi soak, 53
    marshmallow bottle launcher, 128–29
    mint and orange mix, 130–31
    non-mint gum for less snacking, 131
    soda geyser, xii
    sour or acidic candy predictions, 5
    sugar concentration, 21
    taste influences, 131
    toothpaste and taste, 131
seizing, chocolate, 46–47
shooting marshmallows, 129
sinking experiments. See density
    experiments
Skittles
    acids and bases experiment, 8–9
    dissolving experiment, 20–21, 30–31
    pH tests, 4–5
Smarties, 136–37
    bubble experiment, 86–89
Snickers bar, density experiment, 62–63
Soda Can Fizzy Candy, 6–7
soda geyser, xii, 86–89
solute, 16
solvent, 16
sour candies experiments, 4–5
Sour Patch Kids, pH tests, 4–5
Starburst GummiBursts, 38
starch, 44
Steve Spangler Geyser Tube, 86
stirring, 16–17

INDEX

straw bending, 94–95
sugar
    brown sugar crystals, 114–15
    concentration, 21, 134–35
    dissolving experiment, 18–19
    light experiments, 96–97
    lowering freezing point, 30, 31
supersaturated solution, 123
swirl lollipop, 22

taffy, 107, 136–37
taste influences, 131
Tic Tacs, 127, 136–37
tooth dissolving, 13
toothpaste and taste, 131
Tootsie Pop, 66–67
Tootsie Roll, 66–67
Twizzlers, 76
Twizzlers Filled Twists, 38

Warheads
    acid and base experiments, 10–13
    bubble experiment, 90–91
    pH tests, 4–5
water
    absorption experiments, 42–45, 48–49
    adding or removing, 40–57
    chocolate seizing experiment, 46–47
    density and floating in, 62–63
    discoloring chocolate, 48–49
    salt in, 52–53, 107
    swirls, 96–97

xylitol
    crystal experiments, 118–23
    light experiments, 96–97

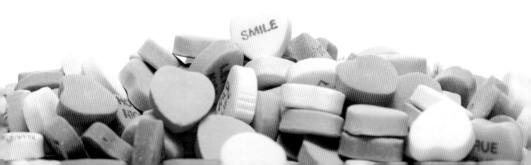

CANDY EXPERIMENTS 2

Andrews McMeel Publishing, LLC
an Andrews McMeel Universal company
1130 Walnut Street, Kansas City, Missouri 64106

www.andrewsmcmeel.com

14 15 16 17 18 SHO 10 9 8 7 6 5 4 3 2 1

ISBN: 978-1-4494-6273-4

All experiments in this book should be performed with adult supervision
by parents or guardians. Neither the author nor the publisher
assumes any responsibility for any injuries or damages arising from any activities.

Made by:
Shanghai Offset Printing Products LTD
Address and place of production:
No. 1320, Xinwei, Liguang Community,
Guanlan Subdistrict, Bao'an District, Shenzhen,
Guangdong Province, China 518110
1st printing — 9/19/14

Attention: Schools and Businesses

Andrews McMeel books are available at quantity discounts with bulk purchase
for educational, business, or sales promotional use. For information, please e-mail
the Andrews McMeel Publishing Special Sales Department:
specialsales@amuniversal.com.

Me, in a PUMA T-shirt, looking skinny but excited about a family vacation. To my left are my dad, my mom, and Ozzie.

Me and Jessica

Walking away from baseball.